CHICAGO STUDIES IN THE HISTORY OF AMERICAN RELIGION

Editors

JERALD C. BRAUER
AND MARTIN E. MARTY

A CARLSON PUBLISHING SERIES

For a complete listing of the titles in this series,
please see the back of this book.

God's People in the Ivory Tower

RELIGION IN THE EARLY AMERICAN UNIVERSITY

Robert S. Shepard

PREFACE BY MARTIN E. MARTY

CARLSON
Publishing Inc

BROOKLYN, NEW YORK, 1991

Please see the end of this volume for a listing of all the titles in the Carlson Publishing Series *Chicago Studies in the History of American Religion*, edited by Jerald C. Brauer and Martin E. Marty, of which this is Volume 20.

Library of Congress Cataloging-in-Publication Data

Shepard, Robert Stephen, 1952—
    God's people in the ivory tower : religion in the early American
university / Robert S. Shepard ; preface by Martin E. Marty.
        p.   cm. — (Chicago studies in the history of American
religion ; 20)
    Includes bibliographical references and index.
    ISBN 0-926019-56-2 (alk. paper)
    1. Religion—Study and teaching—United States—History.
2. Universities and colleges—United States—Religion.   I. Title.
II. Series.
BL41.S535   1991
291'.071'173—dc20   91-26846

Typographic design: Julian Waters

Typeface: Bitstream ITC Galliard

Case design: Alison Lew

Index prepared by Jonathan M. Butler.

Printed on acid-free, 250-year-life paper.

Manufactured in the United States of America.

Contents

An Introduction
to the Series

The *Chicago Studies in the History of American Religion* is a series of books that deal with topics ranging from the time of Jonathan Edwards to the 1970s. Three or four deal with colonial topics and three or four treat the very recent past. About half of them focus on the decades just before and after 1900. One deals with blacks; two concentrate on women. Revivalists, fundamentalists, theologians, life in the suburbs and life in heaven and hell, the Beecher family of old and a monk of new times, Catholics adapting to America and Protestants fighting one another—all these subjects assure that the series has scope. People of every kind of taste and curiosity about American religion will find some books to suit them. Does anything serve to characterize the series as a whole? What does the stamp of "Chicago studies" mean?

Yale historian Sydney Ahlstrom in *A Religious History of the American People*, as influential as any twentieth-century work in its field, pays respect to the "Chicago School" of American religious historians. William Warren Sweet, the pioneer in such studies (beginning in 1927) at Chicago and, in many ways, in America at large represented the culmination of "the Protestant synthesis" in this field. Ahlstrom went on to name two later generations of Chicagoans, including the seminal Sidney E. Mead and major figures like Robert T. Handy and Winthrop Hudson and ending with the two editors of this series. He saw them as often "openly rebellious" in respect to Sweet and his synthesis.

If, as Ahlstrom says, "a disproportionate number" of historians have some connection with the Chicago School, it must be said that the new generation represented in these twenty-one books carries on both the lineage of Sweet and something of the "openly rebellious" character that scholars at Chicago are encouraged to pursue. This means, for one thing, that the "Protestant synthesis" does not characterize their work. These historians question the canon of historical writing produced in the Protestant era even as many of them continue to pursue themes shaped in a Protestant culture. Few of them concentrate on the old "frontier thesis" that marked the early years of the school. The shift for most has been toward the urban and pluralist scene. They call into question, not in devastating rage but in steady patterns of inquiry, the received wisdom about who matters, and why, in American religion.

So it is that this series of books focuses on blacks, women, dispensationalists, suburbanites, members of "marginal" denominations, "ethnics" and immigrants as readily as it does on white men of progressive urban bent in mainstream denominations and of long standing in America. The authors relish religious diversity and enjoy discovering the power of people once considered weak, the centrality to the American plot of those once regarded as peripheral, and the potency of losers who were once disdained by winners. Thus this series enhances an understanding of an America overlooked by the people of Sweet's era two-thirds of a century ago when it all, or most of it, began.

Rebellion for its own sake would not long hold interest; it might tell more about the psychology of rebels and revisers than about their subject matter. Revision, better than rebellion, characterizes the scholars. Re+vision: that's it. There was an original vision that characterized the Chicago School. This was the contention that in secular America and its universities religion mattered, as a theme in the national past and as a presence in the present. Second, it argued that the study of religious history belonged not only in the seminaries and archives of denominations, but also in the rough-and-tumble of the secular university, where no religious meanings were privileged and where each historian had to make a case for the value of his or her story.

Other assumptions from the earliest days pervade the books in this series. They are uncommonly alert to the environment in which expressions of faith occur. That is, they do not take for granted that religion comes protected in self-evidently important and hermetically sealed packages. Churches and denominations are porous, even when they would be sealed off; they cannot be understood apart from the ways the social environs effect them, but their power to effect change in the environment demands equal and truly unapologetic treatment. These writers do not shuffle and mumble and make excuses for their existence or for the choice of apparently arcane subject matter. They try to present their narrative in such ways that they compel attention.

A fourth characteristic that colors these works is a refusal in most cases to be typed in a fashionable slot labeled, variously, "intellectual" or "institutional" history, "cultural" or "social" history, or whatever. While those which concentrate on magisterial thinkers such as Jonathan Edwards are necessarily busy with and devoted to his intellectual achievement, most of the books deal with figures who cannot be understood only as exemplars in a sequence of studies of "the life of the mind." Instead, their biographies and circumstances come very much into play. On the other hand, none of these writers is a reductionist who sees religion as "nothing but" this or that—"nothing but" the working out of believers' Oedipal urges or expressing the economic and class interests of the subjects. Social history becomes in its way intellectual history, even if the intellects are focused on something other than the theologians in the traditions might like to see.

Some years ago *Look* magazine interviewed leaders in various denominations. One was asked if his fellow believers considered that theirs was the only true faith. Yes, he said, but they did not believe that they were the only ones who held it. The editors of this series of studies and the contributors to it do not believe that the "Chicago School," whenever and whatever it was, is the only true approach to American religious history. And, if they did, they would not hold that Chicagoans alone held it. To do so would imply a strange solipsistic or narcissistic impulse that would be the death of collegiality in the historical field. They have welcomed the chance to be in a climate where their inquiries are given such encouragement, where they find a company of fellow scholars in the Divinity School, the History Department, and the Committee on the History of Culture, whence these studies first emerged, and elsewhere in a university that provides a congenial home for massed and massive concentration of a special sort on American religious history.

While the undersigned have been consistently involved, most often together, in all twenty-one books, we want to single out a third person mentioned in so many acknowledgment sections, historian Arthur Mann. He has been a partner in two or three dozen religious history dissertation projects through the years and has been an influential and decisive contributor to the results. We stand in his debt.

Jerald C. Brauer
Martin E. Marty

Editor's Preface

After a revolution has occurred it is hard to imagine how life was before it. New generations cannot picture that there had to be discontent, vision, pioneering, and the making of mistakes before something new could emerge. That part of America which is alert to the religions of the world and that smaller part which takes for granted the study of religion in universities could with good reason assume that such study was as old as universities and that world religions were always part of the curriculum. Of course, the God of Christian faith, of the Bible of Jews and Christians, was the central subject matter of religion teaching in colonial colleges and early national period colleges and universities. But, one might well have thought, especially as America entered a period of international trade and imperial adventure, there must have been academic study of Buddhism, Hinduism, Native American ways, Islam, and the like.

Hardly. The reader of Shepard's book is likely to be surprised at the recency of the revolution in university study of religion. Not until the turn of this century, after higher education had begun to slip away from churchly dominance and when European graduate research models began to hold sway, was the subject of world religion brought up next to world history, geography, or trade. And when it was brought up, few knew what to do with it, or whether to do it. Religion had a hard enough time becoming accepted in tax-supported universities or being honored by a generation of intellectuals which was, in the main, shrugging off the small town religion in which its teachers had been brought up. Comparative or world religion had a harder time.

Why? Robert Shepard, by careful tracing of the experience in the six universities which did most, however little that was, to establish such studies, reveals many of the reasons for the difficulties. For one thing, a practical nation had to ask: what could one do with a world religion major or specialty? Most religious study was theological or ministerial, and graduates who studied Buddhism wanted to do research or teaching, not hold pulpits. The presuppositions of seminary education overwhelmed those who wanted to be "scientific" or "positivist" in their neutrality toward other faiths: Christianity was the true religion over against which others had to be measured negatively. So agents of religious studies had a hard time justifying themselves and their preoccupations.

Far from being self-assured, pre-planned institutions, Boston and Cornell, New York and Pennsylvania, Harvard and Chicago were busy defining themselves. Curriculum was often a hit-and-miss affair, and religious studies had few gifted spokespersons. They could not point to prestigious chairs held by their extremely few Ph.D.s or analogues to prestigious pulpits held by the products of the competitive seminaries down the block. Religionswissenschaft was a young science in Europe, to which graduate seminarists turned for models. So they lacked direction.

Yet Shepard is not telling a story of non-happening but of small beginnings of what has become a large and important enterprise. There were a few early major scholars like Morris Jastrow and George Foot Moore and a few administrators like William Rainey Harper who gave encouragement. There were some students who endured and prevailed over curricular obstacles and went job-hunting, ending up who knows where. And just enough ground work was laid so that when, decades later, permanent structures for inquiry were built, there were reasons for the study of and gratitude to the pioneering institutions and figures whose story Shepard has discovered and so capably told.

Martin E. Marty

God's People in the
Ivory Tower

Introduction

The last quarter of the nineteenth century witnessed a revolution in American higher education. The founding of the Johns Hopkins University in 1876 and the University of Chicago in 1892 illustrate the arrival of a new conception of higher learning, a conception grounded in research, in academic life. Mushrooming specialization of knowledge, the standardization of various institutions forms (e.g., the academic department, degree requirements), and heightened professionalism among the faculty transformed higher education around the country. Laurence Veysey was correct when he wrote, "the fact remains that the American university of 1900 was all but unrecognizable in comparison with the college of 1860."[1]

There were many components to this transformation. Undergraduate enrollment between 1870 and 1890 almost tripled. Yale University awarded the first American Ph.D. in 1861 and in the decades that followed graduate education increased dramatically.[2] By the twentieth century an academic career, accompanied by professional associations, journals, research facilities, and graduate students, was a reality for American scholars. Professional education expanded in scope and authority as the new university became the repository and legitimizer of knowledge particular to the professions of law, medicine, and divinity.[3]

The rise of the American university was, in part, a response to the tremendous changes that took place in post-Civil War society. Some of those changes were intellectual, as the Protestant foundations on which America had been built were shaken by scientific discoveries. The intellectual challenges of Darwinism, biblical criticism, and the study of world religions precipitated a widespread crisis in American religion in the late nineteenth and early twentieth centuries.[4] The new university and its affiliated seminaries provided a setting for the scientific methods that led the attack on the fortress of orthodoxy.

As the traditional structures of Protestantism wobbled under the weight of the challenges just delineated, liberal theology or modernism arose to resolve

1

the conflicts. Discovering a benevolent milieu in such universities and seminaries as Harvard, Yale, Chicago, and Union, scholars at the end of the nineteenth century ushered in what Sydney Ahlstrom has called the "Golden Age of Liberal Theology." Believing that their faith could be adapted to the spirit of the times, liberal theologians, in general, embraced the new methods of science, emphasized humankind's freedom and goodness, promoted moral education, located revelation within the historical process, and were optimistic about humankind's destiny and progress.[5]

The optimism that characterized the liberal theologians was shared by a good portion of the general populace. The social context for much of the scientific scholarly activity was one of acceptance of modern ideas and a desire for unity in religious thought. The most grandiose display of this liberal religious spirit was exhibited at the World's Parliament of Religions held in conjunction with the World's Columbian Exposition in 1893 in Chicago. In a setting of grandeur highlighting the scientific and technical progress of the day, scholars, clergy, and laymen from around the world met to learn more about their respective faiths and seek the unity of purpose that many felt underlaid their differences. The success of the Parliament of Religions illustrated the rising curiosity in world religions and the desire for religious unity.

The advancing interest in world religions was one of the most important challenges facing the turn-of-the-century religious and academic world. As the religions of the globe were made known to scholars and laymen, another threat to the uniqueness of Christianity appeared. Scholars increasingly promulgated the relativistic view that the comparison of religions must be undertaken with no preconception of the truth of any one faith.[6] The approach to religion must be scientific and the universities and seminaries where biblical criticism found a home likewise housed an expanding curriculum in the history and comparison of world religions.

Origins of Religionswissenschaft

The scientific, comparative study of the religions of the globe began in earnest in the latter part of the nineteenth century. Prior to this time religion was customarily seen as a static deposit of faith, unchanging in essentials, given to humankind through divine revelation. The appropriate method of study was to determine the particular contents and directives of the data of revealed religion. Other religions were aberrations of the one divine revelation, a compound of human sin and error. Gradually, however, the attitude of scholars began to change and "the last decades of the nineteenth century saw the first attempt to systematize the material which was emerging from this study [of religion], to subject it to a definite method, and thus to make of it a science."[7]

The new scientific approach did not burst upon the scene ex nihilo. The origins were European as nineteenth-century scientific discoveries throughout the Continent illuminated the religious history of primitive people. The materials to advance the study of religions accumulated rapidly. Archaeological excavations unearthed texts, temple sites, and religious artifacts.[8] Philologists revolutionized linguistic analysis whereby language became the means not only of authenticating literary texts but also of understanding the ethos of primitive cultures.[9] Encompassing all of these methods and discoveries was the evolutionary hypothesis that gave validity to each stage of religious development for all cultures. The resulting method of studying religion, which increasingly gained acceptance, was "scientific, critical, historical, and comparative."[10]

The first significant venture into this new field was undertaken by the German philologist Frederick Max Müller in 1870. His lectures that year at the Royal Institute in London are regarded as the first significant scientific treatment of religion. Published three years later as *Introduction to the Science of Religion, Four Lectures Delivered at the Royal Institute in February and May, 1870*, they signaled the emergence of Religionswissenschaft in Europe. Between 1873 and 1884 seven university chairs were established for the history of religions in various European countries.[11] The first Religionswissenschaft journal, *Revue de l'Histoire des Religions*, was founded in Paris in 1900. The First International Congress for the Science of Religion was held in Stockholm in 1897 and in 1900 the Congrès d'Histoire de Religions convened in Paris. Müller was not alone. He was joined in the task of Religionswissenschaft research by a number of other scholars, the most notable being Dutch Egyptologist and theologian Cornelius Tiele and Albert Reville, professor of the history of religions at the Collège de France.[12]

It did not take long for the new science and its literature to reach North America. The Americans who took interest in the fledgling discipline and promoted it in American universities were well acquainted with the European progress in this field. Many of them had studied in Europe under some of the most renowned Religionswissenschaft scholars of the day. Optimism surrounded the science of religion and American scholars came back buoyed by the prospects of the inroads it could make.

The optimism, in some cases, bordered on fanaticism. Louis Henry Jordan, for example, spent most of his career chronicling the literature, curricular developments, and institutional changes that were relevant to the expanding science of religion. His three major works, *Comparative Religion: Its Genesis and Growth* (1905), *Comparative Religion: A Survey of Its Recent Literature* (1910), and *Comparative Religion: Its Adjuncts and Allies* (1915) provided a wealth of information about the scholarship and institutional settings of Religionswissenschaft research. Although he often exaggerated comparative religion's incursion into and influence on the emerging university, Jordan's enthusiasm for the new science and his belief that comparative religion "can be dealt with adequately only from a university chair"[13] were shared by many American academicians.

The excitement surrounding comparative religion was due in no small part to the growth and prosperity of the research university. The initial emergence of the science of religion coincided with the tremendous expansion and stabilization of many of the modern academic disciplines. The revolution that transformed American higher education in the last quarter of the nineteenth century was accompanied not only by enrollment increases and new methods of scientific research but also by the establishment of research journals, professional associations, and administrative structures that wove the various disciplines into the fabric of academia. The evolution of many of these disciplines at the turn of the century has recently received scholarly attention.[14] Despite initial enthusiasm for comparative religion, it did not experience a similar pattern of growth and professionalization.

Decline of Religionswissenschaft

It is understandable that scholars would look back to the origins of Religionswissenschaft in America after the discipline took root in higher education in the 1950s and 1960s.[15] Willard Oxtoby was correct in 1968 when he claimed that the history of religions had recently prospered in American colleges and universities with the crystallization of a community of Religionswissenschaft scholars.[16] The retrospective looks have, unfortunately, been brief and general.

Joseph Kitagawa was one of the first to point to the disorganized state of affairs in the history of religions in his essay, "The History of Religions in America."[17] Kitagawa viewed the first decades of the twentieth century as being very conducive to comparative and historical studies of religion. The liberal spirit of the times welcomed a scientific approach that sought the unity of all religions. Characterized by the World's Parliament of Religions, a religious liberalism aided the acceptance of comparative religion and the history of religions in universities and seminaries. Unfortunately, with the demise of religious liberalism in the 1930s and the rise of neo-orthodoxy, criticisms began to be leveled against a scientific, historical approach to the study of religion.[18] Kitagawa's most concise statement on this theme is found in his 1983 John Nuveen Lecture at the University of Chicago:

> Despite—or possibly, because of—its lack of clarity as a discipline, the popularity of comparative religion during the first quarter of our century was greatly aided by the spirit of religious liberalism predominant at that time, a spirit which affirmed the oneness of humanity and which had an optimistic vision of social progress. Later, in the 1930's, the sudden decline of comparative religion was accelerated by the impact of neo-orthodox theology, the depression, and the impending war.[19]

In 1959, Erwin R. Goodenough surveyed the field of the history of religions in his presidential address at the founding of the American Society for the Study of Religion.[20] Although his purpose was to outline and promote a revised science of religion, he briefly offered the following reasons why Religionswissenschaft had not flourished in American colleges and universities: (1) American scholars in the late nineteenth century concentrated on the social and ethical teachings of Jesus in pattern with the German theologians Ritschl and Harnack. (2) The Papal Bull of 1912 forbade the analytical method of Religionswissenschaft for Catholics. (3) American scholars' special interest and contribution in applying the new scientific criticism to religion came in the area of psychology and even that was overshadowed with the rise of neo-orthodoxy, which debunked all scientific approaches to religious questions. (4) World War I and the Great Depression of 1929 made a mockery of humankind's scientific efforts and gave cause for a return to revelational religion. Goodenough did not elaborate on or offer evidence to support these generalizations; he merely presented them as part of his theory that after 1914 the scientific study of religion declined rapidly.

One of the most comprehensive works on comparative religion is Eric Sharpe's *Comparative Religion: A History*, published in 1975. Sharpe likewise discovered the complex rise and fall of Religionswissenschaft and presented his own account of the amazing decline of the discipline.

> In effect, the situation of comparative religion in America at the turn of the century, modifying factors notwithstanding, did not differ fundamentally from that obtaining in many parts of Europe at the same time. The same elements—motive, material and method—were in evidence. . . . Eventually, comparative religion was to suffer something of an eclipse, despite its promising beginnings, under the pressures of conservatism and orthodoxy.[21]

The rise of neo-orthodoxy, the impending war and depression, the decline of religious liberalism, and the struggle with conservatism—these are the reasons most often offered for the desuetude of American Religionswissenschaft after World War I. There is no doubt some truth in each of these interpretations, but all are generalizations given by scholars taking a casual glance at the past. There has been no attempt at substantive analysis of the rise and decline of the nascent discipline in American universities and thus there exists a real gap in our historical knowledge. This book attempts to narrow that gap through a comparative analysis of the institutional settings that nurtured but did not wean the academic field of comparative religion.

The Response of American Universities

The intellectual history of any discipline certainly makes an important contribution to knowledge. Historical analyses of the changing presuppositions and methodologies of fields of knowledge are significant and in regard to the science of religion the question of an appropriate methodology has been one of the most common concerns.[22] My interest, however, is in the broader question of the relationship of knowledge to its social context. Scholars do not formulate ideas, publish those ideas, or seek funding to discover new ideas in a vacuum. In order to understand the scholarship that infiltrated and aided the formation of modern universities the full range of personal, institutional, and social influences must be understood.[23]

This work uncovers the social context of the emerging Religionswissenschaft in American universities at the turn of the century. As social history, it examines the institutional settings where the new discipline first received support. The vision of university leadership for the new science, the conditions surrounding the appointments of Religionswissenschaft scholars and their attempts to advance the discipline, the interest the field held for students, and the curricular and degree structures that were initiated for the study of the science of religion all receive attention.

The institutions treated are six. Boston University, the University of Chicago, Cornell University, Harvard Divinity School, New York University, and the University of Pennsylvania all committed themselves to the new science of religion by establishing professorships or academic programs in the nascent discipline. There is little doubt that Harvard and Chicago held the most potential for the institutional blossoming of Religionswissenschaft. Both universities had the wealth, prestige, and scholarly resources to become Religionswissenschaft centers and to serve as models for other institutions less inclined to commit to the fledgling and untested discipline. Harvard's long commitment to the study of world religions and its appointment of George Foot Moore in 1904 as Frothingham Professor of the History of Religions provided it with a strong Religionswissenschaft reputation. Chicago's initiation of a Ph.D. in comparative religion from the university's opening solidified its role as a front-runner in the promotion of the science of religion. The strength, reputation, and active Religionswissenschaft programs of these two universities dictate a more extensive assessment of their institutional environments. Boston University, Cornell University, New York University, and the University of Pennsylvania can be treated in broader strokes. All six universities, nonetheless, were acknowledged by scholars at the turn of the century to have made significant provision for comparative religion.

A word of explanation is in order about the use of the term Religionswissenschaft. In no way do I imply a hermeneutical orientation to the study of religion as popularized by the famous historian of religion, Mircea Eliade. The scientific study of religion that originated in the last quarter of the nineteenth century was objective and historical. It usually took one of two institutional forms or designations, comparative religion or the history of religions. Relevant scholars and institutions did not significantly distinguish between the two. Unless specifically stated otherwise, I treat both under the general rubric of the science of religion, or Religionswissenschaft.

In the intermingling of personal, institutional, and social forces that shaped American Religionswissenschaft lies the story of its role in higher education. This book is a comparative analysis of six academic environments whose nourishment was crucial to the development of the science of religion. The inchoateness and weakness of the field is not adequately explained by the generalized reasons previously reviewed. The institutional and social environments of the people who tried to push ahead the discipline must be taken into account. By doing so this work tells a story that has never been told—the rise and decline of American Religionswissenschaft—and contributes to understanding the social context of one of the branches of knowledge seeking status in American universities at the turn of the century.

ONE

The Bleakness of the Educational Landscape

Louis Henry Jordan's exhaustive survey of the inroads of the science of comparative religion in his *Comparative Religion: Its Genesis and Growth* contained a summary of the colleges and universities throughout the world that had provided for the new discipline. His printed queries to American institutions of higher learning revealed that five universities purported to have a chair "for imparting instruction in Comparative Religion": Boston University, the University of Chicago, Cornell University, New York University, and Brown University.[1]

Had Jordan distributed his surveys a decade later the University of Pennsylvania would have likewise received mention in his book. The research of Morris Jastrow and his organization of the history of religions program at Penn made a remarkable contribution. Although many colleges and seminaries experimented with a few courses on Religionswissenschaft, the four institutions treated in this chapter demonstrated their commitment to the new science by establishing chairs or programs of study in response to the growing excitement.

The men who led the Religionswissenschaft charge at Boston University, Cornell University, New York University, and the University of Pennsylvania—William F. Warren, Charles Mellen Tyler, Frank F. Ellinwood, and Morris Jastrow, Jr., respectively—differed greatly in terms of educational background, research interests, and Religionswissenschaft identity. Moreover, the institutions represented by these men illustrate the widely divergent patterns of emergence of the history of religions or comparative religion as a course of study. The social and institutional contexts of these four scholars illustrate the irregularity and fragility of the American university's interest in the scientific study of religion and thereby the bleakness of the educational landscape for the flourishing of the nascent field.

Boston University

On May 26, 1869, three prominent Boston business and civic leaders were granted the charter that established Boston University. Jacob Sleeper, Lee Claflin, and Isaac Rich, all Methodist laymen, called on William Fairfield Warren to lead their new educational institution. Warren had been president of the Methodist-affiliated Boston Theological School since 1867 and was both a friend of the three founders and a highly respected theologian and Methodist lay leader.

From the beginning Boston University was to be private and nonsectarian. Section five of its Act of Incorporation read as follows:

> No instructor in said university shall ever be required by the trustees to profess any particular religious opinions as a test for office, and no student shall be refused admission to, or denied any of the privileges, honors, or degrees of said university on account of the religious opinions which he may entertain; but this section shall not apply to the Theological Department of said university.[2]

The exclusion of theological studies from the nonsectarian domain of the university revealed an underlying Methodist orientation. The theological school, a training ground for Methodist ministers and missionaries, became the first department of the university in 1871. Within the next three years six additional schools and colleges were added. Although explicitly nondenominational, these units took on the Methodist spirit that could and did expressly characterize the School of Theology. In the College of Liberal Arts (1873), for example, the first two deans were ordained ministers of the Methodist Episcopal Church and the third was a Methodist layman. Most of the faculty and students were Methodists and official university representation was secured at the annual denominational meetings of the Methodist Social Union. As Warren Ault stated in his history of Boston University's College of Liberal Arts, "Nonetheless, there was a good deal that was Methodist about the college in the first half century of its history."[3] The strength of the Methodist tradition was most strongly represented by the fact that the first five presidents of Boston University, 1869-1967, were all ordained Methodist ministers.

The driving intellectual and organizational force behind Boston University's first thirty-four years was its president, William F. Warren. Warren graduated from Wesleyan University in 1853 at the age of twenty and soon after became an ordained minister of the Methodist Episcopal Church. After a short term with parishes in and around Boston, Warren traveled to Europe where he studied at the University of Berlin and the University of Halle in 1856 and 1857. His love of scholarship, and particularly German theological scholarship, evidenced itself in his acceptance of a professorship in systematic theology at the Missionsanstalt in Bremen, Germany. Holding the post from 1861 to 1866, Warren wrote a number of articles and books on theological topics in English and German. By the time of his return to the United States in 1867 and his assumption of the presidency of the Boston Theological School, he was well known in theological circles, particularly within the Methodist community.

While in Europe, Warren had a chance to reflect on the relationship of science and the university to the church and theology. He embraced the scientific methods of biblical criticism that he encountered in Germany and became firmly committed to the ideals of scientific research. He also, nevertheless, felt that theology had a rightful place in the university and that the church should be able to have a say in the affairs of the theological departments that would supply its ministers. In June 1857, from Germany, Warren wrote in the *Christian Advocate and Journal*,

> Science has emancipated herself from the thraldom of the Church, and dearly too. . . . Let her enjoy her hard won liberty. I only wish to maintain that, if the Church is compelled by political relations to make use of the public universities for the education of the clergy, she ought of right to have a word to say as to who shall and who shall not occupy the theological chairs; who of those educated there shall and who shall not be inducted into her pulpits.[4]

This belief in the rightful power of the church was no doubt the cause of the exclusion of the theological school from nondenominational status in the university's 1869 Act of Incorporation. It also enabled Warren to invite the Methodist Episcopal conference periodically to examine the work of the School of Theology.[5]

Warren believed that in addition to the church's proper role in the university, theology was to be valued for its liberating and educative powers. Religion was not to be immune from the penetrating, scientific eye of the researcher. It was to be analyzed and treated like all sciences and when so scrutinized its liberating and uplifting powers would be unharnessed. The same norms of scholarship applied to theologian and scientist. The historic, philosophic, and systematic study of religion and theology was the goal; the result was a liberated mind. In his 1880-81 annual report Warren summarized his thinking:

> The value of the study of Theology as a quickening, broadening, and liberalizing discipline has seldom, if ever, found due recognition. . . . Whether one contemplates the subject matter of the study [theology], its relative dignity or breadth or importance, or normal influence upon the mind investigating it; or whether one examines the numberless and most intimate relations of the theological sciences to all others; or whether one looks at the kind and power of the motives and sympathies legitimately brought into activity in the learner,—the pre-eminently broadening and quickening influence of the theological discipline cannot be doubted. . . . A university afraid of theology is like a Naturforscher who is afraid of astronomy.[6]

Warren's study in Europe and abiding interest in the frontiers of theological scholarship had acquainted him with the nascent discipline of comparative religion. He gained an expertise in the field of ancient religion and cosmology. His most highly regarded scholarly works were *The True Key to Ancient Cosmology and Mythical Geography* (1882), *Paradise Found* (1885), and *The Earliest Cosmologies* (1909). His research in ancient conceptions of the universe combined with a fascination for the religions of the world to produce a series of lectures and courses on comparative religion that he gave throughout his thirty-four-year tenure as president—and simultaneously professor in the theological school—of Boston University. In 1873, due to Warren's influence, the university established a professorship of comparative theology, and of the history and philosophy of religion. Although the title of the chair changed slightly over the subsequent three decades, Warren was always the holder.

Warren was always quick to remind listeners and readers that Boston's 1873 professorship was the first in the United States devoted to the historic and scientific study of religions of the world. In his twentieth annual report he traced the history of the university's commitment to world religions to the course Religions of India, given in 1867-68. The 1873 comparative theology professorship was, according to Warren, "the first distinct and regular chair provided for this study [comparative theology and religion] in America."[7] As occupant of the chair, it was Warren's practice to offer two courses, Comparative Theology and Comparative Religion. When he resigned from Boston's presidency in 1902 to take a year of study in Europe, the Board of

Trustees, in Warren's honor, renamed the chair the Warren Professorship of Comparative Religion and of the History and Philosophy of Religion.

Warren's course in comparative religion was extremely popular with students and well known in the ecclesiastical community of Boston. In 1911, at the urging of friends, students, and associates, Warren published an outline of his lectures entitled *The Religions of the World and the World-Religion*. The outline followed the course sequence as offered at Boston University and included the divisions Introduction to the Scientific Study of Religious Phenomena, History of Religions and of Religion, Descriptive Exposition of Religions and of Religion, and the Philosophy of Religion. Warren hoped that the scheme would provide collegiate and seminary professors of comparative religion or the philosophy of religion the use of

> a time-saving device in explaining to neophytes the genesis and scope of the branch of instruction engaging their immediate attention, and especially its proper place in the one organism which involves and integrates all as yet defined and elaborated sciences relating to religion.[8]

It is not surprising that Warren's manual made laudatory reference to the work of the great historians of his day. The works of Tiele, de la Saussaye, and Jastrow, among others, were cited.[9] He gave a lengthy polemic on the need for the scientific method in the study of religion. Nevertheless, Warren remained committed to the ultimate supremacy of the Christian faith as both a starting point and the natural culmination of scientific inquiry into religion. In the preface he proudly wrote that he began from the perspective of Christian theism, of which there was nothing "higher, deeper, or more scientific." The modern methods of research were to be practiced by all faithful students of religion, and when the student investigated, in a scientific spirit, the world's religions,

> The height and depth and length and breadth of God's kingdom are seen in a light never dreamed of before. Now for the first time does Christianity become the true World-Religion, the explanation of all history, the prophecy of the yet-to-be-consummated ethnic and cosmic unity.[10]

Warren's university embraced theology, his theology welcomed science, and his science culminated in Christianity.

It was only natural for Warren to place comparative religion academically and administratively under the jurisdiction of the School of Theology. Religion and theology were to be studied scientifically within the context of theological education. There was no thought of making comparative religion a separate and distinct unit of study with its own academic degree. It was one of six or seven departments of instruction in the School of Theology during the first few decades of the school's existence. Although students from the college could take comparative religion courses, the vast majority of enrollments in Warren's courses were undergraduate theological students.

The students studying comparative religion under Warren were part of an enrollment explosion at Boston University from 1885 to 1895. The university's overall enrollment increased from 620 to 1,252. During the same period attendance in the School of Theology rose from 79 to 152 and by 1908 enrollment had surpassed 200, more than at any other divinity school in the United States at the time.

This influx of students contributed to the growth and success of Warren's courses. He occasionally complained about the difficulty of teaching a subject as comprehensive as comparative religion to classes of over fifty students. Despite the increasing numbers, the students were of only two types: ministers (or prospective ministers) and missionaries who were studying to receive their bachelor of sacred theology degrees. There were few potential scholars of Religionswissenschaft as there was neither an undergraduate major in comparative religion nor a related graduate program to pursue.

Although Warren often touted the scientific nature and method of his treatment of world religions, the substance of his course and its attractiveness to the students and constituents of Boston University were grounded firmly in Christian apologetic motives and ministerial utility. This was most clearly seen in the public pronouncements about Warren's chair in comparative religion and its value. In the June 7, 1893 issue of *Zion's Herald*, for example, the following review of Warren's course on The Religions of the World and the World-Religion was given:

> The value of such a line of instruction is manifest. The public teacher of religion cannot be too familiar with the history and state of religion the whole world over. Missionaries on furlough attending the course have repeatedly expressed their high appreciation of its value. It has helped to make some of the best missionaries now in the service of the church. It has rooted and grounded the faith of many a wavering mind. It prevents the young minister from being imposed upon by unscholarly dabblers who write in the magazines or lecture in the lyceums on ethnic religions. . . . It furnishes the only broad and scientific basis for the defense of the Christian faith.[11]

14

The ministerial vocation of the students of Boston University's School of Theology is confirmed by a look through the dean's annual reports in the years approximating the arrival of the twentieth century. In 1891, for example, Dean Buell reported that the theological school graduated twenty-six men, all of whom, with one exception, entered the pastorate. The same trend held in 1896 when all but three of the 143 students enrolled were "candidates for the Christian ministry." The dean's report for 1896 also confirmed that many of the students immediately entered the ministry: "All of the graduates [38 at the June 1896 commencement] except one, who is continuing his studies, are already pastors of churches."[12]

The School of Theology did, nevertheless, excite and encourage some of its students to pursue graduate study. Dean Buell proudly announced in his report for the 1889-90 academic year that no less than seven recent graduates had traveled to Europe to pursue an advanced course of study. The theology faculty played a role by deciding that a number of courses would count toward the fulfillment of requirements for the Ph.D. from Boston's graduate school. However, nothing significant was undertaken academically or administratively to redirect the school from its primary mission of ministerial education. When the doctor of sacred theology degree was instituted in 1890, for example, it did not require the extensive research and scholarly achievement that typified doctoral requirements at other universities. The first regulation approved by the trustees granted the degree to all S.T.B. graduates of Boston University of not less than ten years' standing.[13] At both the graduate (S.T.D.) and undergraduate (S.T.B.) level, comparative religion remained a welcome and necessary handmaiden to the theological study that was to prepare minister and missionary for the work of the "World-Religion."

Although committed to rigorous academic methods under the leadership of Warren, Boston University's School of Theology always also remained alive to the ideals of the practical and vocational elements of a prospective minister's education. Courses in Christian missions, urban problems, and the psychology of religion rounded out the theological school's curriculum. In the first two decades of the twentieth century the administration increasingly sought to demonstrate the university's utility for the problems of a growing and changing Boston metropolis. Lemuel H. Murlin, for example, the third president of Boston University, devoted his inaugural address in 1911 to the influence and role of the university, including the School of Theology, within the city.[14] The School of Theology shared this deepening concern for utility through its propensity to emphasize the practical side of Christianity. Richard Cameron, in his history of Boston University's School of Theology, has stated,

> The tendency to stress the practical side of Christianity, and the applicability of the Seminary's courses to the work of the minister and the daily lives of his people was not, of course, confined to the period [1911-1926] we are to consider in this chapter, but perhaps there never was a period when they were more nearly dominant than then.[15]

It was within this social and institutional context that Warren taught his final class in comparative religion in 1919. The appropriateness of the scientific method for theology and the rightful place of theology within the university for which Warren had long argued had been realized in many ways. The issue of the utility of theological education now loomed in the forefront and with comparative religion ensconced in the seminary courses in world religions became melded with related courses in missions. Such a merger was not peculiar considering that Warren's offerings in comparative religion were often promoted for their value and usefulness for missionaries or prospective missionaries.

In the years immediately after Warren relinquished his teaching responsibilities at Boston, courses in the history of religions and comparative religion were shuttled between a number of professors. The first year, 1919-1920, Henry Sheldon, professor of systematic theology, taught two related courses and students were referred to the Department of Missions for additional work. Then, in 1920-1921, Francis Strickland, professor of the history and psychology of religion, offered coursework in non-Christian religions in addition to his primary interest in the psychology of religion. Strickland was shortly thereafter relieved of his duties in the history of religions so that he could concentrate on the psychology of religion.

With the reorganization of the curriculum in 1925-1926, comparative religion was given a place that would keep it secure for the decades that followed. The theological school's program of study was divided into five "Group Plans" according to the different needs for preparation for the various types of ministry. Plan number three was the Missionary Group, which required twelve hours of study in missions and non-Christian religions. Comparative Religion thus had been officially assigned the role of broadening the perspective of potential missionaries and, through course elections, ministers.

Cornell University

It was only fitting that the university established by Ezra Cornell should bear, from its opening, the same liberal religious spirit that characterized its founder. Ezra Cornell, a Quaker by birth, was openly disdainful of petty theological disputes and sectarian bickering. His religion was one of devotion to the Almighty without denominational narrowness. Andrew D. White, Cornell University's first president, remarked about Ezra Cornell:

> He had been born into the Society of Friends, and their quietness, simplicity, freedom from noisy activities, and devotion to the public good, attached him to them. But his was not a bigoted attachment; he went freely to various churches, aiding them without distinction of sect, though finally he settled into a steady attendance at the Unitarian Church in Ithaca, for the pastor of which he conceived a great respect and liking.[16]

When Cornell University opened its doors on October 8, 1868, its charter stipulated that the constitution of the Board of Trustees would be such "that at no time shall a majority thereof be of any one religious sect, or of no religious sect" and furthermore, in regard to the university proper, "Persons of every or no religious denomination shall be equally eligible to all offices and appointments." This nonsectarianism brought harsh criticism from the religious press and conservative churchmen. Andrew D. White, himself not immune from attacks on his orthodoxy,[17] was often and mightily confronted with defending the university against charges of godlessness. He chose to answer such indictments clearly and forcibly from the first moments of his presidency. In his inaugural address he boldly announced that sectarianism had restricted both academic freedom and the funding possibilities of denominational colleges. He stated simply, "the sectarian spirit has been the worst foe of enlarged university education."[18]

Andrew White's and Ezra Cornell's nondenominationalism was not, despite charges to the contrary, unbridled secularism. Both men considered themselves believers in the "essentials" of Christianity. The university they established was likewise committed to the promotion of Christian ideals within its academic framework. The first General Announcement published by Cornell expressed the highest aim of the university as the promotion of Christian civilization. Ezra Cornell spoke to the point when he declared at the proceedings of the university's inaugural day, "It shall be our aim and our constant effort to make true Christian men, without dwarfing or paring them down to fit the narrow gauge of any sect."[19]

The Morrill Land Grant Act of 1862 was the major catalyst that motivated White and Cornell to action when both were New York State senators and led, ultimately, to the founding of the university. White wanted a university of the first order and was not content that it be limited, in the words of the Morrill Act, to instruction in "agriculture and mechanic arts." Ezra Cornell agreed with White and when the bill that established the university was signed on April 27, 1865, it stated that in addition to the promotion of agriculture, mechanical arts, and military tactics for the industrial classes, "such other branches of science and knowledge may be embraced in the plan of instruction and investigation pertaining to the university as the trustees may deem useful and proper."[20]

This broader purpose enabled White immediately to hire the Reverend William Dexter Wilson as professor of moral and intellectual philosophy. A graduate of Harvard Divinity School in 1838 and a Unitarian minister, Wilson lectured at Cornell during its first eighteen years on psychology, logic, moral philosophy, the history of philosophy, and the philosophy of history. This was the entire philosophical curriculum offered at the university until 1886 and laid the groundwork for Cornell's brief flirtation with the science of religion.

Most attempts to assure the Christian orientation of the university and its students took place outside the classroom. On June 13, 1875, Sage Chapel, named for philanthropist and friend of the university Henry W. Sage, was dedicated. Immediately thereafter Dean Sage, Henry's son, expressed his desire to provide an endowment to support a university chaplaincy, preferably restricted to an Episcopal clergyman. Sage was afraid that without proper controls the chaplaincy might come to propagate doctrines inconsistent with accepted theories of Christianity. Andrew White remained steadfast in his resolve to allow no sectarianism to creep into the university and finally persuaded Dean Sage to endow a fund for $30,000 that would bring preachers of all denominations to speak in Sage Chapel to students and townspeople. White and other Cornell University loyalists often referred to Sage Chapel and the Sage preacherships—along with the work of the University Christian Association—to disprove the "irreligion" of Cornell.[21]

Henry W. Sage, however, was not content to allow the Christian foundation of the university to be left to occasional visits of preachers who spoke at chapel services that were not mandatory for the religiously needy student body. He desired to make a strong impact on the religious and moral lives of students by endowing a professorship of ethics and philosophy. He had a special fondness for philosophy, which he viewed as the inculcator of Christian morality. In January 1886, he announced the establishment of the Susan E. Linn Sage Professorship of Christian Ethics and Mental Philosophy in memory of his wife, who died tragically in July 1885. Sage's intent was clear:

> my chief object in founding this professorship is to secure to Cornell University for all coming time the services of a teacher who shall instruct students in mental philosophy and ethics from a definitely Christian standpoint.[22]

A young philosopher, Jacob Gould Schurman, was chosen as the first holder of the Sage professorship and his brilliance as a lecturer and author soon became evident. Student registrations increased and another instructor was added to the department. Courses in ethics, metaphysics, Kant's critical philosophy, and English empirical philosophy joined the standard offerings in psychology, logic, and philosophy. Most important, Henry W. Sage took a strong liking to Jacob Schurman and his work.

In October 1890, Henry Sage decided to put philosophy and ethics on a permanently sound footing by endowing an entire school of philosophy with a gift of $200,000. The university was required to add other funds to support the work and Jacob Schurman was appointed the dean of the newly named Susan Linn Sage School of Philosophy. The reasons behind Sage's interest in philosophy had not changed, as his letter announcing the charitable gift made clear. After claiming Cornell had not done enough to uplift the moral and religious elements of its students, Sage wrote,

> Our function here is to educate man, and through education to provide foundation of character, based on moral principle, which shall underlie the whole man, and give impulse, tone and color to all the work of his life. . . . No education can be complete which does not carry forward, with the acquisition of knowledge for his intellectual side and physical wants, a broad and thorough cultivation of his moral and religious side, developing Christian virtues, veneration, benevolence, conscience, a sense of duty to God and man, purity and right living in the largest sense.[23]

Sage's desire for a "Christian" school of philosophy did not signify a retreat from the best and most successful developments taking place in the field of philosophy throughout the world. Dean Jacob Schurman, at Sage's request, spent a few months in Europe studying the organization and methods of instruction of the philosophy departments of British and German universities. Upon his return he recommended the establishment of a psychological laboratory, the incorporation of pedagogy as a subject matter, and a more liberal provision for traditional fields of philosophy. Also, and most important, he suggested a chair for the history and philosophy of religion. It was later added that the chair would also teach Christian ethics, a provision no doubt required by Henry W. Sage.

It was generally acknowledged that Cornell's new professorship in the history and philosophy of religion and Christianity ethics represented a significant advance for the growing discipline of Religionswissenschaft in America. The internationally known historian of religion Jean Reville, in an article that charted the progress and diffusion of the history of religions, highlighted Cornell's "special chair for the teaching of the history of religions."[24] Louis H. Jordan remarked that "it was not perhaps until 1891, when a Chair was formally set apart to this work [comparative religion] in Cornell University, that the American movement can be said to have distinctly begun."[25] Morris Jastrow, although also optimistic, wondered whether the additional responsibility for Christian ethics would hinder the full treatment the history of religion so strongly deserved and restrict the research agenda of the chair's occupant.[26]

No matter what the judgment concerning the chair's potential, Schurman did not seek a top scholar to fill the position. Although he would have desired such an opportunity, he was too politic to oppose the wishes of the generous but shortsighted Henry W. Sage. In 1881 Sage had proposed that the pastor of his Congregational church in Ithaca, Reverend Charles Mellen Tyler, be appointed professor of ancient history at Cornell. That appointment was averted, but the new professorship in the history and philosophy of religion recommended by Schurman gave Sage another chance. In 1891 the Susan Linn Sage School of Philosophy officially opened with the Reverend Charles Tyler as the Sage Professor of the History and Philosophy of Religion and of Christian Ethics.

Charles Mellen Tyler graduated from Yale College in 1855. After a year of study at Union Theological Seminary he was ordained into the ministry of the Congregational Church and subsequently held pastorates in Illinois, Massachusetts, and Ithaca. A chaplain during the Civil War, Tyler also briefly served as a member of the Massachusetts General Court.

Tyler had a fondness for literature and history and read widely in the field of Christian ethics. Although he wrote a number of articles and one theological book, *Bases of Religious Belief, Historic and Ideal* (1897), he had no formal training and pursued little original research in the field of comparative religion. His doctor of divinity degree from Yale was honorary. He was neither a crusader for the new science of religion nor an original thinker in the discipline. Hewitt remarked in his discussion of the origins of Cornell's chair in the history and philosophy of religion and of Christian ethics, "In order that the subjects embraced in it might correspond to the previous studies of Professor Tyler, the subject of Christian ethics was added."[27]

When the Sage School of Philosophy opened in 1891 Tyler was one of eight faculty members. For the following twelve years he taught courses in applied ethics, the history of religions, and the philosophy of religion. He also offered a seminar for advanced students in the history and philosophy of religion. Although the latter seminar, according to the *1898-99 Cornell University Register*, was "for graduate students who have undertaken theses on the history or the philosophy of religion," not a single graduate student wrote a thesis on a topic related to the history of religion. (It is doubtful whether Tyler would have been able to provide much guidance for such a student anyway.) The doctorates awarded from the Department of Philosophy between 1891 and 1903 (in 1903 Tyler became professor emeritus) were in the more traditional fields of philosophy and psychology and the subsequent teaching careers of the graduates revealed this orientation.[28]

Administered as part of the Sage School of Philosophy without a distinct program or degree and tied to a benefactor-influenced concern with Christian ethics, it is doubtful whether the history of religion would have been successful at Cornell even if Tyler had been a foremost Religionswissenschaft scholar. In the 1905-6 register, the Sage School proudly proclaimed that among the ten members of its instructing corps was "a professor of the history and philosophy of religion." It failed to mention that Tyler was emeritus and the following year there was no listing of the professorship in the history and philosophy of religion. Tyler's courses in applied ethics and the history of religion were not replaced and his seminar was dropped. Tyler's influence, as little as it may have been, diminished immediately. The brief incursion of the science of religion was simply a small part of the work of the Sage School of Philosophy and the school easily continued without it upon Tyler's retirement.

New York University

When New York University was incorporated in 1831, its nonsectarian status was resolutely proclaimed. All offices and appointments in the university were open equally to persons of every religious denomination and no one religious sect was to control the governing board through a majority of members.[29] This plan, presented and discussed in the years immediately preceding the incorporation, sparked considerable debate in New York's influential Christian community. The fear that the nonsectarian nature of New York University would assure its secularism led to a public announcement on January 15, 1830, in the New York City newspapers. A standing committee reported that even though the university's nonsectarianism precluded a faculty of theology, from time to time teachers of different denominations would be appointed to offer instruction in practical religion and the evidences of Christianity.[30] The same statutes that instituted the nonsectarian basis of the university also called for the establishment of a professorship in evidences of revealed religion.

The tension between New York's nonsectarianism and the desire to remain in some sense distinctively Christian permeated the university throughout the nineteenth century. In January 1850, the Reverend Cyrus Mason resigned his professorship in evidences of revealed religion and with his resignation the endowed chair collapsed. Jones's history of New York University tells us that most of the endowment had, in any case, been spent on the completion of the university chapel.[31] Apparently filling the gap caused by the dissolution of this chair, a professorship of evangelical theology was established. Nevertheless, the proper role and function of this position increasingly came under scrutiny. By 1870 the council (trustees) recommended

> That the Professorship of Evangelical Theology be, with the consent of Mr. Andrews, abolished, as unnecessary in a city where Theological seminaries can much more thoroughly furnish theological instruction, and as conflicting practically with the basis on which the University is founded.[32]

Few students availed themselves of the opportunity to take the handful of religion courses offered during New York University's first fifty years. The related professorships did, however, provide Chancellor Henry MacCracken with a precedent when he lifted the university from the quagmire of mediocrity and made possible a graduate program in comparative religion.

Dr. Henry MacCracken, the first full-time vice-chancellor of New York University (1885-1890) and subsequently the chancellor (1890-1910), played a formative role in the institution's progress and growth. After the Civil War the university had fallen on difficult times. Student enrollments had dwindled and the means to improve instruction and expand facilities had not materialized. The undergraduate program was particularly weak. In 1885 the university was still granting the A.M. degree without examination upon alumni who applied for it. These situations Henry MacCracken gradually corrected. Despite not having the necessary endowment, he hired new faculty members and initiated a graduate program with requirements in keeping with the standards employed at respected universities. Theodore Jones concluded:

> Within the first five years of his [MacCracken's] entrance into office, therefore, the new Vice-Chancellor had made himself a living force throughout the whole University, which for the first time since its foundation gave evidence of integration and progress.[33]

MacCracken was a religious man with close ties to the Presbyterian synod of New York. His interest in the religious life of the student body was expressed through support for a strong YMCA program and required daily chapel. In his 1901 quadrennial report he devoted an entire chapter to the religious work of the university and proudly proclaimed the university was doing its Christian duty for students.

MacCracken's religious interests often took on sectarian overtones. There was, in fact, a suspicion that he wanted to convert the university into a sectarian school. As early as 1887, he invited the Presbyterian synod of New York to visit and inspect the campus. The faculty was to "lend them every aid in securing the information they may desire respecting our collegiate work"[34] and the synod committee submitted a report on their findings and recommendations that was published in the university's 1888 annual report. This practice continued for many years and occasionally resulted in some controversial advice. For example, after their 1893 visit the synod committee suggested:

> This form of religious teaching, now maintained under limited means, presents a very strong claim for the complete endowment of a chair that should divide its time between graduates and undergraduates—thus lifting the Holy Scriptures and their religion to a position of recognized prime importance. The animus of

our national government is undoubtedly Christian; and our institutions of learning may justly magnify the Christian element in their courses of study.[35]

The sectarian tendencies of MacCracken were more than likely an attempt to gain important benefactors for the university. In his annual reports he often invited visitation committees from any neighboring synod or conference to examine the programs of New York University. His 1888 annual report, moreover, explicitly asked, "Is not the time near when we must . . . approach the denomination which has taken us into correspondence, and seek to secure by its machinery the raising of money for this Christian University?"[36]

The Protestant ethos that MacCracken championed at New York University, although tempered by a sensitivity to the university's nonsectarian history,[37] gave him opportunity to provide for the religious instruction of students through the hiring of appropriate faculty. MacCracken was well aware that even though a theological school could never be an official part of the university, a number of ministers and prospective ministers were taking courses under his faculty's tutelage. In his 1897 annual report he remarked that visiting committees from ecclesiastical bodies were free to inspect and report on the work of New York University because, "Not a few students are with us who are looking forward to becoming ministers in the Presbyterian, Methodist Episcopal, Protestant Episcopal, Reformed, Lutheran, Congregational or Baptist Churches."[38] MacCracken seized the opportunity to raise the level of the graduate school within the university and in 1886, the same year the graduate school was reorganized, he hired Abram S. Isaacs, a Jew, to teach graduate courses in Hebrew. The following year he appointed Frank F. Ellinwood, a Presbyterian, as professor of comparative religion.

Frank Ellinwood, as did many of the men in the late nineteenth century who took an interest in comparative religion or the history of religions, had an early start in the ministry. He completed undergraduate study at Hamilton College in 1849 and in 1853 was graduated from Princeton Theological Seminary. The pastorate followed immediately; first at the Second Presbyterian Church of Belvidere, New Jersey, and a year later at the Central Presbyterian Church of Rochester, New York. Unlike many of the people who studied the new science of religion at that time, however, Ellinwood neither studied abroad nor received a Ph.D. in a related discipline. Ill health necessitated his retirement from the pastorate in 1865 and he spent the rest of his life in various administrative positions with the Presbyterian Church. His two higher degrees were honorary awards. In 1865 he received the doctor of divinity degree from New York University and the doctor of laws was awarded in 1895 from the same institution.

In 1871 Ellinwood was called to the secretaryship of the Presbyterian Board of Foreign Missions, a position he continued to hold while teaching at New York from 1887 to 1904. From his mission work he gained an interest in the comparison of Christianity to the world's religions and in his lifetime published many magazine articles on this theme as well as three books, *The Great Conquest* (1877), *Oriental Religions and Christianity* (1892), and *Questions and Phases of Modern Missions* (1899).

There is no doubt that Ellinwood was an apologist for the superiority of Christianity. Although desirous of giving other religions fair and serious treatment (his meaning of the word *scientific*), he claimed that the careful examination of other faiths would demonstrate the supremacy of the words and actions of Christ. In a synopsis of one of Ellinwood's first lectures at the university, published in *The University Quarterly*, the author summarized Ellinwood's discussion of Oriental religions:

> But a comparative study of religions of the Sacred Books of the East, only confirms the Christian scholar in the belief that the noblest precepts of these books are relics of the truth once given by God to all mankind, but from which heathen nations have apostatized.[39]

The author concluded by claiming Ellinwood said, "I do not disguise the fact that I shall consider the subject from a Christian standpoint. I maintain that in discussions of this kind a perfectly colorless, opinionless attitude is impossible."[40]

Ellinwood's perspective found few enemies during his tenure at New York University. This was due in large part to the fact that nearly all of his students were either pastors or candidates for the Christian ministry. After fifteen years of teaching he admitted that of the approximately three hundred students who had taken his courses most were ministers representing every denomination.[41] More to the point, in his 1894-95 annual report he commented on the type of student he commanded and his objective in teaching comparative religion:

> The men who apply for my courses are all of one class, clergymen *in esse* or *in posse* who are moved mainly by the desire to fit themselves to grapple with the new science of Comparative Religion which has brought all the faiths of the world to the front and even into aggressive propagandism at our doors. . . . I try to cultivate in the student a habit of scientific treatment of religion as of

everything else. Faraday complained forty years ago that in all the English educational processes there was no education of the judgment and that it was for that reason that spiritualism and a thousand other follies took such hold on seemingly intelligent people. I would like to train our young ministers to study the laws of evidence, to prove all things, to avoid every sort of sophistry, and in all cases to know what they affirm.[42]

There was little intention on the part of Ellinwood or MacCracken to initiate a graduate program in comparative religion that would train scholars to engage in serious research in the science of religion. The comparative religion program in MacCracken's university was organized to provide ministers with a chance to further their theological education. When Ellinwood's first course in comparative religion was announced in a supplement to the 1887-88 catalog, the orientation of the course and the type of students desired was made explicit:

> In answer to a request for instruction in the great Pagan Philosophies and Theologies, the University Council sought the services of someone specially familiar with this field. The consent of many named Dr. Ellinwood. . . . The course will be so directed as to serve non-resident graduates.[43]

The theological orientation of courses in comparative religion and related areas of study bothered some of the faculty who desired a more scientific, academic approach and objective in a university that claimed to be nonsectarian. Abram Isaacs, for one, desired to teach Hebrew in the graduate school from a historical and scientific perspective. He realized dangers involved in doing so in a Christian environment but nevertheless made the following request to MacCracken in September 1905:

> The idea occurs to me that I might assume charge of a number of courses in the Semitic dept. of the Graduate Seminary [graduate school], depending of course on fees alone—for one year only as an experiment. This would give me a hold upon our community and enable me to ask aid with more confidence, while it would be a partial test of the popularity of Semitic work at the University, which has been restricted, I fear, by young theologians. I wish to lay stress on Hebrew as *literature*, not theology, which is apt to frighten away all but a few.[44]

MacCracken's and Ellinwood's intention to attract ministers into the graduate school was supported by the university's policy of waiving tuition fees for the often financially strapped pastors. Unlike Charles Eliot's attempt at Harvard to raise the divinity school tuition to a level comparable with other divisions and schools within the university, MacCracken's initiation of examinations and other degree requirements in New York's graduate school carried no provision that students in comparative religion pay the standard tuition fee. Although this arrangement allowed many men to take courses with Frank Ellinwood who otherwise may not have been able to do so, it had the undesirable consequence of shortchanging Ellinwood, whose salary was dependent, as was the salary of most of the graduate faculty, on student fees. The situation got so bad that in 1890 MacCracken recommended in his annual report that an additional $10,000 be raised for endowment to support instruction in comparative religion.

The $10,000 endowment was to be a supplement to a previous gift that established in March 1890 the Benjamin F. Butler Chair in Comparative Religion. Vice-Chancellor MacCracken in 1889 had told the council of the university of the imperative and immediate need of $200,000. Charles Butler, president of the council, responded with a contribution of $100,000. Part of this gift went to establish the Benjamin F. Butler Chair in Comparative Religion, named in memory of Charles's brother Benjamin, who had been the first law professor in the university. The importance of the Butler chair was that it represented the commitment of Butler and MacCracken to ease the financial burden of Ellinwood and continue the flow of theological students into New York University. An endowed chair in comparative religion would help close the gap between needed resources and the free tuition afforded ministers and theological students. There was no design to support a strong academic program in the emerging discipline of Religionswissenschaft. The reasons behind the endowment of the Butler chair were practical and financial.

With the giving of large sums of money often comes an opportunity to exert power and influence. In the case of Charles Butler, his contribution enabled him at the same time to ask for an alliance between Union Theological Seminary and New York University. Butler was also president of the Board of Trustees at Union and for over fifty years had played an active role in both institutions. A few weeks after announcing the final $80,000 of his $100,000 pledge to New York University, Butler convened a meeting with committees from Union and New York to complete an agreement. He expressed openly and officially his desire

to have a connection effected between the Union Theological Seminary of the City of New York, and the University of the City of New York which may be of mutual advantage giving to each greater distinction and greater power of influence in the work of Christian education.[45]

The terms of agreement were adopted on April 1, 1890, with only one Union Theological Seminary committee member abstaining from the vote.[46] The terms of the alliance permitted seminary students to be admitted, without fee and upon consent of the professor concerned, to graduate courses in the university. The seminary, likewise, was to register, without fee, graduate students of the university. Most important, however, was the provision which allowed the university to confer the degree of bachelor of divinity upon seminary students recommended by the faculty and trustees of Union. Nonsectarian New York University was thus able to award a divinity degree without having a theological school.

The alliance brought with it a number of problems. The first was the increase in the number of nonpaying students. Ellinwood was especially vulnerable because his courses were filled with seminary students and ministers. MacCracken continued to seek subscriptions and endowment funds to supplement Ellinwood's menial pay. The question also arose as to requirements and fees for seminary students who wished to take examinations for the master's or doctor's degrees. In his 1890 annual report MacCracken announced that a fee would be imposed but referred the issue of the amount to a committee in the graduate school.

Although the alliance between Union Theological Seminary and New York University brought a great number of Union students to New York's comparative religion courses, it did not bring about the central intent of the plan, namely, the establishment of New York University's role as provider of bachelor of divinity degrees. Merely six years after the articles of agreement were adopted the alliance was dissolved. Not a single bachelor of divinity degree had been granted. In a terse letter to MacCracken, Union president Thomas S. Hastings summarized the feelings of Union's faculty and trustees:

> The statement you saw in the Tribune was correct. Our Board of Directors was not unmindful of the courteous offer of the University to confer the degree of B.D. on our recommendation. Columbia University also had the matter under consideration. But our Faculty & Board thought it better that we should ourselves be authorized to confer the degree. Learning that the power to authorize us to do this is now vested in the Regents of the State, I had some correspondence with them which resulted in their agreement to confer the degree on our high-grade men on our recommendation. The Faculty & Board

agreed upon this as an experiment. If not satisfactory we shall apply for power to confer the degree ourselves.[47]

Union's desire for independence did not deter New York University from attracting theological students of all denominations into its halls. It is important to note that the growth of the graduate school near the end of the nineteenth century was due in no small part to the influx of theological students. In 1894, for example, over one third of the graduate students were registered in Ellinwood's comparative religion courses. Far from shutting out Union Seminary students after the termination of the alliance, New York University continued to admit them without fees. Moreover, both the exemption from tuition fees and the granting of seminary credit toward New York University degrees were extended to all theological seminaries in the proximity of the university, including General Theological Seminary, Princeton, Drew, and New Brunswick. Ellinwood and MacCracken continued to provide relevant theological courses to seminary men and women and, occasionally, enroll them in university degree programs. There was never a concern to develop a Religionswissenschaft graduate program to attract scholars. The intention was to provide the necessary ingredients to ensure the growth of a Christian university that would increasingly attract a Christian student body and constituency.

The six-year alliance with Union Theological Seminary notwithstanding, New York University never attempted to establish a theological school or merge with an existing one. Its courses in comparative religion were initially offered in the philosophy and history group in the graduate school and when the number of groups was expanded to seven in 1912, comparative religion found a home in a group entitled Philosophy and Religion. The number of courses offered never reached more than three, with Ellinwood typically teaching one per semester. Charles G. Shaw of the philosophy department occasionally supplemented Ellinwood's work with a course on the philosophy of religion or the history of religious thought.

The graduate school experienced tremendous growth during the first thirty years of its existence. In 1886-87, 15 students were enrolled and by 1914-15, 409 men and women matriculated in one of seven graduate groups of study. The number of doctorates awarded between 1887 and 1914 was 246; importantly, 94 were earned by clergymen.

The few ministers who completed the Ph.D. with an emphasis in comparative religion did so under the tutelage of Ellinwood. Unfortunately, his part-time status, poor health, and retirement in 1903 all combined to produce a weak program.[48] Specifically, four men, three pastors and one church administrator, received their doctorates in comparative religion between 1893 and 1901. In 1893 Lindsay Parker, pastor of the Amity Baptist Church in Brooklyn, received his Ph.D. with a thesis entitled "Gautama Buddha and Jesus Christ as Moral Teachers." One year later Eleander Jamison, pastor of the Methodist Episcopal Church in Andover, New Jersey, was awarded the doctorate for a dissertation entitled "The Non-Biblical Faiths Represented at the Parliament of Religions and Their Contrasts with Christianity." George William Carter followed in 1900, after writing a thesis on "A Comparison Between Zoroastrianism and Judaism." (Carter was secretary of the New York Bible Society.) Finally, in 1901 Andrew Beattie, pastor of the Calvary Baptist Church in Berkeley, California, received the final Ph.D. in comparative religion awarded during those years. He wrote his dissertation on "Confucianism."

It is not surprising that a number of ministers decided to pursue the Ph.D. at New York University, considering the intent of MacCracken and Ellinwood to attract such students. The majority received their degrees in the fields of languages, church history, or philosophy.[49] It is also understandable that with MacCracken's retirement in 1909 and the subsequent initiation of tuition fees for theological students the number of doctorates awarded to clergymen rapidly declined. By 1914 only four of the nineteen Ph.D.s awarded were earned by clergymen. The student growth within the secular disciplines in the first two decades of the twentieth century at New York University was contrasted by the relative decline in students and studies in theological areas.

When Ellinwood resigned in 1903, the decision was made to add the title Butler Lecturer in Comparative Religion to assistant professor of philosophy Charles G. Shaw. Shaw never, however, taught a course in comparative religion. His interest in the philosophy of religion and his liberalism frightened away the conservative ministers wooed to New York University by the ever-popular Ellinwood. Shaw continued the Butler Chair in Comparative Religion in name only and by 1929 his title as Butler Lecturer was dropped.

Frank F. Ellinwood's influence on the ministers who took his course was profound. One student wrote to him as follows:

> I desire to express to you my high appreciation of the course of study in heathen religions and philosophies, through which I have gone with you during the past year. It has seemed to me one of the most helpful post-graduate lines of work that a minister can possibly take. The facts and thoughts which it presents are almost or quite essential to pulpit work. . . . Incidentally it furnishes an

inexhaustible fund of illustration for pulpit use. I speak from the standpoint of a minister in active work—it is a most delightful side study, interweaving itself with every line of pulpit effort.[50]

This illustrates the type of student Ellinwood and MacCracken proudly sought and around whom they organized the course of study in comparative religion.

University of Pennsylvania

The religious toleration that characterized the colonial Quakers and the Pennsylvania territories they occupied—including Philadelphia—likewise accompanied the founding of the University of Pennsylvania. In 1749 Benjamin Franklin published an essay entitled "Proposals Relating to the Education of Youth in Pennsylvania," which led in the same year to the drafting of a set of "Constitutions for a Public Academy in the City of Philadelphia" by Franklin and Tench Francis, attorney general of the province. These "Constitutions" were adopted in November 1749 by twenty-four trustees who had made subscriptions in support of the academy and in 1753 the first charter was granted for what was to become the University of Pennsylvania.[51]

The scarce mention of religion in Franklin's "Proposals" and the "Constitutions" stands in stark contrast to the traditions of the founding of other colonial colleges about the same time. There was no provision for the training of a learned ministry for any particular denomination. Furthermore, the trustees were to be selected "without regard to difference of religious persuasion." There would be no sectarianism. In governance and purpose the Philadelphia Academy was founded on secular and radically new grounds. As Edward Potts Cheyney stated in his history of the University of Pennsylvania:

> Educational institutions had in the past been established by groups of masters or of students for the mere love of learning, as were the medieval universities, or by religious societies for training their ministers or educating the young within their own fold, or by sovereigns to increase their prestige. The Philadelphia Academy was different from all these. It was established by a "voluntary society of founders," as they long afterward called themselves, for purely secular and civic purposes, without the support of any religious body or the patronage of any person or government.[52]

The religious toleration and nonsectarianism of the University of Pennsylvania played a significant role in the historical dearth of theological curricula. Of great importance was the fact that no divinity school affiliated or merged with the growing institution. Although Protestant clergy were amply represented on the faculty and many undergraduates did, as one would expect, seek ministerial careers, few courses and no formal program of study in religion appeared at Penn until the twentieth century.

The exclusion of theology from the curriculum carried with it a benefit. When Oriental studies and other Religionswissenschaft-related academic programs were established at Pennsylvania in the late nineteenth century, they began as scientifically grounded academic offerings and not as adjuncts to professional or preprofessional programs for ministers. Even the Semitics department and the teaching of Hebrew were offered with little concern for the training of the clergy. Cyrus H. Gordon, in his history of the Semitics department at Pennsylvania, claimed:

> By excluding theology, Franklin predetermined that when the University of Pennsylvania came of age and would have a Semitics department, it would be in accordance with the standards of two sciences, yet to be born: archaeology and linguistics; but theology would not influence its development.[53]

That theology played such a minor role in terms of curricular influence at Penn should not be taken to imply an absence of a Protestant ethos or dearth of ministers or theological students matriculating in various academic programs. Until the middle of the nineteenth century, all of the Pennsylvania provosts and many faculty were Protestant clergymen. Gordon referred to the fact that Penn's aversion to Hebrew as a theological course of study was problematic because, "A sizable proportion of the study body planned to enter the Protestant ministry, and in those days, any divinity school worthy of the name required Hebrew as a prerequisite for advanced work."[54] In the academic year 1902-3, responding to the needs of some of its students, the Semitics department offered three courses in Old Testament, "planned with especial reference to the interest of theological students and ministers of all denominations."[55]

It is nevertheless true that Oriental studies generally and Semitics specifically at Penn were founded on the newly discovered scientific principles of philology and linguistics. The secular basis for the growth of Oriental studies was transported from Europe where many of Penn's Oriental scholars studied in the late nineteenth century. It was this grounding and orientation that provided the framework for the genesis of the history of religions program in 1910.

The University of Pennsylvania became the American center for the study of Near Eastern languages and cultures near the end of the nineteenth century. Pennsylvania faculty members John P. Peters and Hermann V. Hilprecht led expeditions to Nippur in 1888-89 and 1889-90 that yielded extremely important inscribed tablets and artifacts. Later trips produced more texts and monuments, and a university museum was established to house some of the artifacts and publish the findings of the Nippur expeditions. Penn was able to attract a number of prominent Assyriologists, archaeologists, and Semitists, who were drawn to it as a center for Near Eastern scholarship. One of the most polymathic Oriental scholars of the Pennsylvania faculty, and the man who established the Semitics program, was Morris Jastrow, Jr.

Jastrow was the son of a distinguished and respected Philadelphia rabbi, Marcus Jastrow. Morris Jastrow received his early training in private schools and in 1881 graduated with a bachelor of arts degree from the University of Pennsylvania. He immediately left for Europe, where he encountered many of the world's most famous Semitists and Orientalists. In Germany he studied with Franz and Friedrich Delitzsch and in France with Ernest Renan. His original intention was to follow in his father's footsteps in the rabbinate and from 1881 to 1884 he attended the Jewish Theological Seminary at Breslau. During this time he also studied at the University of Leipzig and received his doctorate from Leipzig in 1884.

Of no small consequence for Jastrow's later interest in the history of religions was his occasion to study in Europe with the famous historian of religion, Cornelius P. Tiele. Tiele held the history and philosophy of religion chair at the University of Leiden in Holland and was one of Europe's earliest and most famous scholars to apply scientific principles to the study of religion. His appointment in 1877 was regarded as the first Religionswissenschaft position in Europe and his popularity with the Dutch government led to the establishment of three other university chairs in the historical study of religions in Dutch cities.

Tiele's profound influence on the young Jastrow was evident from Jastrow's publication of two articles to commemorate the work and influence of Tiele, one on the occasion of the latter's seventieth birthday and one just after his death.[56] Remembering him as "the leading authority on the science of religions," Jastrow also gave Tiele credit for introducing the history of religion into the university curriculum. Jastrow's tutelage under Tiele meant that when the Philadelphian returned from Europe he was not only proficient in Hebrew, Aramaic, Assyriology, and other Semitic languages, but he also had gained a start in the history of religions. Cyrus Gordon commented:

> In addition to learning Semitics, including Assyriology, from the greatest living masters [in Europe], Jastrow became involved in the new field of comparative religions. This was important for his future service at Penn, where teaching one's own religion was taboo, but where, for that very reason, the objective study of comparative religions was a desideratum.[57]

Upon his return to Philadelphia in 1885, Jastrow decided not to complete an apprenticeship at his father's Rodef Shalom congregation and thereby to avoid the rabbinate.[58] He accepted a position as instructor in Semitics at the University of Pennsylvania that same year and in 1891 was appointed professor of Semitics, which enabled him to establish Penn's first Semitics program.

Jastrow's range of course offerings in Semitics and Oriental languages was extraordinary. During his tenure at Penn he taught classes in Hebrew, Aramaic, Arabic, Assyrian, and Syriac, to name a few. He was well aware of the advances of Semitic studies in higher education in the United States and claimed early in his career that the "outlook for the future of Semitic studies is indeed promising."[59] He was active in leadership positions in the Oriental Club of Philadelphia, the American Oriental Society, and the Society of Biblical Literature. At Penn, when the Semitic languages program was organized in the Department of Philosophy (graduate school) in 1897-98, Jastrow was appointed chairman.[60] He remained an active voice in the affairs of the department until his death in 1921 and supervised the studies of many of the graduate students who eventually received their Ph.D.'s in Semitics.[61]

Concomitant with Jastrow's involvement and interest in Semitics was his abiding zeal for the emerging field of the history of religions. As early as 1893, only two years after his appointment as professor of Semitics, he published an article that reviewed the progress of Religionswissenschaft in America.[62] His summary of American universities that had provided for the new discipline revealed both a close acquaintance with the related research of other colleagues and scholars and a curiosity to investigate the inroads of the history of religions at places unfamiliar. He could scarcely contain his optimism when he wrote, "Taking the past as an augur of the future, we may confidently look forward to seeing at an early day fully equipped departments for the historical study of religions established at our leading universities."[63]

Jastrow's early writings on the need for and place of the history of religions also disclosed an awareness of the structure the new science would need to take within the research university in order to succeed. His European experience gave him a perspective from which he organized his hypothetical department of the history of religions. Although Harvard, Penn, and Chicago had set an example by introducing Religionswissenschaft courses, more was needed:

> But in order that the historical study of religions may be carried on in accord with the method above outlined, something more than a number of courses or even a special chair is demanded. The French Government has recognized that by means of a special department alone can satisfactory results be attained. . . . On the other hand, a defect of the French school consists in its failure to furnish that broad illustration from the various fields that have been shown to be essential to a complete study. . . . To meet the practical objections that may be raised against so apparently extensive a scheme, it may be pointed out that the larger universities of this country, with special chairs already established for the study of the various Ancient Languages, and with equipment for Anthropological and Psychological researches, are in a position with but little additional expense to create such a department as is here in view.[64]

Jastrow did more than any other American scholar to promulgate the historical method as the sine qua non of the study of religion and to promote the study of the history of religions in American universities and society. His *Study of Religion*, published in 1901, was a superb polemic for the use of objective and scientific methods and was widely used as an introductory textbook. In 1898 he organized a section of the American Oriental Society for "The Historical Study of Religions" and as secretary of the American Committee on the History of Religions he helped organize lectures by eminent scholars on Religionswissenschaft topics. He also edited a series of handbooks on the history of religions and served as one of the official delegates of the United States government to the Third and Fourth International Congresses for the History of Religion held at Oxford and Leiden.[65] When George A. Barton, Jastrow's successor at Penn, wrote Jastrow's biography for the *Dictionary of American Biography*, he rightfully claimed, "Few American scholars have done as much as he to promote interest in the study of the history of religion."[66]

Jastrow did not allow his own institution to bypass its responsibility for the nascent discipline of the history of religions. In his aforementioned article that chronicled the inroads of Religionswissenschaft, he related that Penn had welcomed the subject by offering five courses in the university curriculum.[67] The *1894-95 Catalogue* confirmed that five courses under the history of religions subdivision of the division of philosophy, history, and political economy in the Department of Philosophy were presented. Inexplicably, both the courses and the subdivision vanished the following year. Then, in the academic year 1910-11, Jastrow's wish was fulfilled. The history of religions was officially recognized as one of the twenty "Groups" in which graduate programs of study were offered. A student could choose the history of religions as either a major or a minor and could receive a Ph.D. in the field.

There is little doubt that serious scholarship was the objective of the history of religions group. Ministerial training had no formal role to play. Nothing had changed since the *1894-95 Catalogue* announced:

> The object aimed at [for graduate students] is not only an advance in knowledge, but also an initiation into the proper method of pursuing scientific study and research. So conducted, the instruction is especially valuable to those who wish to devote themselves to scientific research as well as those who wish to become teachers.[68]

Jastrow and his colleagues who formed the history of religions group sought serious students and researchers.

In organizing the group for the historical study of religions, Jastrow attempted to come as close to his ideal Religionswissenschaft department, as presented earlier, as possible. He needed to provide both breadth and depth to his students and therefore sought the cooperation of a number of his fellow Pennsylvania faculty in related fields. A spring 1910 survey to his colleagues revealed a strong interest in Jastrow's plan and enabled the organization of a group committee to map out a course arrangement to cover adequately the discipline for the student major or minor. Eleven men joined Jastrow on the group committee: Morton W. Easton (comparative philology), William R. Newbold (moral philosophy), Walton B. McDaniel (Latin), Arthur C. Howland (medieval history), George B. Gordon (anthropology), Roland G. Kent (comparative philology), James A. Montgomery (Semitics), Edward M. Fogel (Germanics), George D. Hadzsits (Latin), W. Max Muller (Egyptology), and Clark D. Lamberton (classics).

In 1910-11 fifteen courses were presented by the group. Jastrow lectured on Outline of the History of Religions and committed himself to teach Introduction to the Study of Religions the following year. Other courses on primitive religions, religion of the Hebrews, Christian archaeology, early church history, and the history of Greek ethical theories, to give a few examples, rounded out the program of study. In general the candidate for the doctor's degree was to fulfill two conditions: first, a thorough acquaintance with the broad issues of the history of religions for comparative purposes, and second, the mastery of one religion or a group of religions as a specialist with an emphasis on knowledge of the original sources. Prospective students were to consult with the professor in charge of the major subject for specific course arrangements and degree requirements.

Jastrow chose the University of Pennsylvania student newspaper *Old Penn* to summarize the entrance of Religionswissenschaft into the Pennsylvania curriculum. In the March 1, 1911 issue, he traced the program's origin to the success of an initial course offering, Introduction to the History of Religions, in 1908. (He made no mention of the courses offered in 1894-95!) Almost twenty students enrolled in that class and the following year a similarly favorable attendance marked a General Outlines to the History of Religions course. It then "became manifest that for an adequate recognition provision should be made to enable students to select the historical study of religions also as a major."[69] The cooperation of other Penn scholars was secured and the group for the history of religions was formed. Jastrow emphasized that it was important that the study of religions at Penn be handled scientifically. Too often at other places, he claimed, Religionswissenschaft had fallen into the hands of the dilettanti and insufficiently equipped students. His goal was to "maintain for this field the same high standards that mark the Graduate School as a whole."[70]

Jastrow was optimistic that his new graduate group would attract students. In his *Old Penn* article he announced that nine students had selected the history of religions as a major field of study and another nine had chosen it as their minor field. With the discipline "now fully recognized and introduced" it was to have little difficulty attracting increasing numbers of students. The group did, in fact, award two doctorates in the first five years of its existence.[71] In 1912 James J. Watson received his Ph.D. in the history of religion with a dissertation entitled "The Religion of the Negro." He was followed by Richard E. Clark, whose doctoral degree was awarded in 1915 with the thesis "The Effect of Social Forces upon Religious Rites and Ceremonies." Watson subsequently returned to the South and took over the proprietorship of the East Albany Warehouse Company in Albany, Georgia. Clark became a professor of political and social science at Coker College in Hartsville, South Carolina.

These two men were, however, the exception. Although a number of students chose the history of religions as a minor field, few committed themselves to its rigors for the reward of a doctorate. Between 1915 and 1924 no other Ph.D.'s were given in the discipline. Although course registrations were generally ample, they reflected the opportunity for Semitics, Germanics, and philology students to take elective courses in Religionswissenschaft.

Morris Jastrow took a leave of absence from Pennsylvania for the academic year 1921-22. On June 22, 1921, he died. His imprint on the history of religions at Penn was unmistakable. Jastrow had organized a program that trained students in religion in accord with the most scientific, objective, and historical methods. Many of his fellow faculty in related fields had caught his excitement for the fledgling discipline.[72] His death marked the passing of an era and was severely felt in the struggling history of religions group.

The University of Pennsylvania acting provost report for 1920-21 stated simply, "Professor George A. Barton has recently been elected to fill the vacancy caused by the death of Professor Jastrow, one of our most eminent scholars."[73] Barton was hired as professor of Semitics to chair the Semitic languages and archaeology group of the graduate school. Although not as polymathic as Jastrow, he nevertheless taught a wide range of subjects including Egyptology, Assyriology, Old and New Testament, history of religions, and archaeology.

Simultaneously holding the position of professor of New Testament at nearby Philadelphia Divinity School, Barton initially continued Jastrow's course offerings on Introduction to the Study of Religion and Outline of the History of Religions. It soon became apparent, however, that the history of religions held neither the attraction nor the excitement for Barton that it had for Jastrow.[74] Barton led the history of religions group in a plan of closer cooperation with surrounding divinity schools in order to procure lecturers in the history of religion. Within three years after Jastrow's death the Religionswissenschaft courses introduced by him were being taught by visiting faculty from surrounding divinity schools.[75] The identity and cohesiveness of the history of religions group deteriorated and it became a haven for ministers and rabbis of proximate churches and synagogues to continue their studies.[76] It is revealing that when Barton retired in 1932-33, Penn faculty member

John K. Shryock continued the history of religions tradition started by Jastrow by offering the course Outline of Non-Christian Religions, a course Jastrow would undoubtedly have placed outside the proper sphere of Religionswissenschaft.

TWO

The Vision for Religion
in the University:
Harper and Eliot

The antebellum college was founded on piety and the cultivation of the learned gentleman. The old-time curriculum, Hebrew, Latin, and Greek included, sought the training of impressionable minds and the discipline of the occasionally wayward spirit. Such efforts had a psychological and moral basis, but were fundamentally grounded in Christian theology as the raison d'être for the structure, substance, and spirit of a collegiate education. Laurence Veysey reminds us that the history of the antebellum college was "closely bound to the history of American religion."[1]

The challenge of Darwinism and the scientific discoveries that shook the Protestant foundations of American society in the final quarter of the nineteenth century helped to unseat theology from its central place in higher education. Theological subjects were overshadowed by a knowledge explosion that added courses and disciplines in rapid succession, a vocational and practical approach to higher education that increasingly gained acceptance, and the growth of professional education with its incumbent need for preprofessional (nontheological) training.

The academic revolution that created the new research university and transformed the old-time college was in a distinctive way driven by a coterie of strong-willed men whose academic leadership created a new administrative bureaucracy.[2] The rise of presidential authority within this new structure is too obvious to need elaboration; Charles W. Eliot at Harvard, William Rainey Harper at Chicago, Nicholas Murray Butler at Columbia, Daniel Coit Gilman at Hopkins, James B. Angell at Michigan, and Andrew D. White at Cornell all played a formative role in the growth of their respective institutions. There is little wonder that expressions such as "academic empire-builders" have been used to characterize the university presidents of this era.[3]

As Christian theology began to lose its hold on American higher education, the captains of new educational enterprises were forced to find a new way to justify the inclusion of theology or religion in the academic mission of the university. Although some presidents concentrated on improving the religious life of the student body, others adopted an emerging conception that gave theology a rightful place in the academic world. William Rainey Harper and Charles Eliot were two such presidents who provided an academic structure for the scholarly treatment of religion, at Chicago and Harvard respectively. More important, however, they promulgated a new rationale, a new conception of the place of religious studies in the academic environment. It was this new vision that drove their decisions to give Religionswissenschaft a corner of their educational empires.

William Rainey Harper

In death, a person often becomes larger than life. Imperfections of character have no place in eulogy. In June 1906, Professor E. H. Lewis of the University of Chicago memorialized President William Rainey Harper in a convocation ode read at the university's 1906 convocation. The ode concluded:

> Hebraic-minded in Teutonic frame,
> Great toiler, builder great, and greater friend,
> Creative hope, aspiring like a flame,
> Wielder of power to power's most noble end,
> Live, live in us, brave spirit, teaching still
> The broader vision and the braver act.
> And in that valley of the staff and rod,
> Teach us the hero's will,
> Who smiles from lips by human anguish racked,
> And dies firm trusting in a human God.[4]

William Rainey Harper's role in shaping the University of Chicago into one of the nation's premier universities and in changing the contours of higher education generally is inescapable. It is hardly possible to overestimate the influence of Harper and his vision for the origin and growth of the University of Chicago. Even when he was alive, Harper's indispensability in leading the new university was acknowledged. John D. Rockefeller, the university's munificent founder, stated at the decennial convocation on June 18, 1901, that had it not been for President Harper the University of Chicago "would not be in existence today."[5]

Harper's imprint on the university raises a number of questions related to the place of religion and religious studies at the burgeoning institution. What place did the academic study of religion have in the context of the religious education of the student body? Did Harper embrace and officially recognize the scientific study of religion? What role, if any, was the divinity school to play in providing for Religionswissenschaft?

A. The University and Religious Education

Let there be no mistake about the fact that William Rainey Harper created a university free from ecclesiastical control. Despite the University of Chicago's origins in the American Baptist Education Society, Harper remained committed to the university ideals of self-government and freedom of expression.[6] Religious authorities would not direct the course of the university, and religion, embodied in ecclesiastical garb, had no formal role to play. In an 1899 speech entitled "The University and Democracy," Harper stated, "That institution cannot become a university, or remain one, which to any considerable extent is controlled by a power other than that which proceeds from within itself."[7] Harper added, "The three birthmarks of a university are, therefore, self-government, freedom from ecclesiastical control, and the right of free utterance."[8]

Harper's disagreement with tight clerical control did not, however, signify his rejection of a religious purpose for the educational enterprise he was building. He spoke candidly and frequently of the importance of the religious education of the student body and the need for a religious purpose for the university. In a series of talks to students in 1904, later printed in book form, he said, "I am more confident today than ever before that the universities and colleges are not performing their full function in the matter of religious education."[9]

Harper's vision for the religious but not sectarian purpose of higher education was derived from his conception of religion. Although a committed Christian, Harper preferred to use the term more as a descriptive adjective than a limiting noun. Jesus Christ was the final and fullest revelation of God, but all religions shared in the revealed truth. As might be expected from a biblical scholar, Harper's understanding of religion and its role in life resulted from a keen analysis of Scripture.

One of the more enlightening interpretations of William Rainey Harper and the scriptural basis that drove his vision for the university is found in a 1983 University of Chicago dissertation by James Wind entitled "The Bible and the University: The Messianic Vision of William Rainey Harper."[10] Wind claimed there was an integrating vision in Harper's work underlying all of his conceptions about the role of the university in society. Harper's vision was derived through the scholarly study of Hebrew scriptures, which in turn elevated the Bible to a place of prominence. A new biblical perspective, founded on critical scholarship, unveiled a God who was at work in human history. This God, most perfectly expressed in the life and work of Jesus Christ, was lifting humanity to a higher moral and spiritual level. The university became an instrument in God's uplifting of humankind.

According to Wind, Harper's mission was to remake America into a model of the biblical world and thereby reach everyone with the truth. There was no conflict between religious faith and the mission of the university. The university, in fact, was the Messiah. Higher education, and for that matter all of education, was one of the means by which God would accomplish his will in the new democratic society. The university was Harper's new mediating institution for religious knowledge.

> . . . the university, in its grappling with the great problems of the ages, was to suffer for society, for the world, in order that all might ascend to higher life. Ultimately Harper's vision was messianic. He traced the messianic idea from its prophetic origins up to his present moment; indeed Harper could claim—without the Old Testament scholar inside of him wincing—that the university was "Messiah."[11]

Harper's most explicit statement on the relationship of religion to society and the university is found in his *Religion and the Higher Life*. Defining the "higher life" as a life associated with moral and righteous behavior, Harper sketched his understanding of the relationship of religion to the other branches of knowledge. Religion took an all-encompassing role as being "essential for the fullest development of these phases of the higher life."[12] Not to be confounded with or separated from art, science, philosophy, or ethics, religion was the guiding force that gave coherence and meaning to the other spheres of life. Philosophers or scientists who believed they could understand the elements of the universe without regard to religion were deluding themselves. Harper stated, "All this, we can see, is equivalent to saying that in working for the highest and fullest and truest development one must not ignore religion."[13]

It was in this context that Harper was able to claim a rightful place for religion within higher education. Just as religion encompassed all of human knowledge, so too should the university provide for the cultivation of a religious spirit that was the basis for all truth. The religious spirit did not contradict the scientific spirit; both sought the fundamental truth of things. The close alliance between religion as the higher life and religion as encompassing all of human knowledge allows one to understand more fully Harper's claim that "just as there rests upon each of us as an individual the obligation to cultivate the religious spirit, there rests also upon us as a university the obligation to cultivate the religious spirit."[14]

Harper did not return to the antebellum college practice of requiring a moral philosophy or religion course of all graduating seniors to serve as the capstone course that integrated religion with all previous subjects studied. Neither did he assume that all instructors would instinctively observe in their subjects the all-encompassing nature of religion. Rather, he advocated the inclusion in the curriculum of courses touching on the religious life. Such courses included but were not limited to biblical languages, biblical history and literature, psychology, pedagogy, sociology, philosophy, ethics, and comparative religion. Harper's purpose was not to start a debate as to which academic subjects held more "religious" potential. He simply believed that whereas the university was the new mediator of all knowledge, including religious knowledge, it had justifiably within its role the religious education of students; and this religious education was to be scientific, research-oriented, and part of the standard curriculum. Some subjects were to touch directly on issues of religion, but all had to recognize their ultimate basis in religion. Storr was correct when he claimed that Harper's perspective about the role of the university "implied belief that it was in service to the cause of religion that the University would find its ultimate fulfillment and most nearly perfect unity."[15]

B. The University of Chicago Divinity School

The religious purpose basic to the entire university did not preclude the need for a division or department that would specifically treat the fundamental questions of religion and train religious leaders. The original subscription of John D. Rockefeller of $1 million to establish the University of Chicago stipulated that the Baptist Union Theological Seminary of Chicago was to become the divinity school of the new university. Harper's vision of the role and place of the divinity school further illuminated his thinking on the theoretical and practical aspects of religion in higher education.

Harper's new agenda for theological education had its roots in the difficulties he saw in the church and its affiliated seminaries. Harper frequently spoke out against the antiquated approaches of the seminaries of his day, which merely mimicked the traditions of their respective denominations. Seminaries had lost touch with modern life. In "The University and Religious Education," Harper stated emphatically, "It is doubtful whether in the last fifty years a single important problem relating to the religious life and education has been solved in the theological seminaries of the United States."[16]

Harper's remedy for the sickness of theological education was an openness to the modern spirit that would revolutionize the profession of the ministry and bring the critical interpretation of Scripture to center stage. Harper's reforms were made at a time when theological education in America was undergoing a transformation. Although a comprehensive history of American seminary education has not been written, Robert W. Lynn has sketched the outline of such a history in his unpublished "Notes Toward a History: Theological Encyclopedia and the Evolution of American Seminary Curriculum, 1808-1968."[17] Lynn saw Harper's reforms as precursors to many of the later developments in twentieth-century theological education. Harper led the revolt against an antiquated seminary education.

Harper's most explicit statement on the form and function of his reformed divinity school is found in an essay entitled "Shall the Theological Curriculum Be Modified, and How?"[18] After reviewing the deplorable state of the theological seminary of that day, Harper proposed two guiding principles that were to form the groundwork for modifications in the seminary curriculum. The first revealed his continuing adherence to modern science. Harper claimed that "the first [principle] is that modifications of the curriculum should accord with the assured results of modern psychology and pedagogy."[19] These new sciences had made significant discoveries concerning human behavior and the learning process. The seminary had to make way for a society that was rapidly adjusting to new scientific discoveries.

The second principle was that modifications in the curriculum should be based on the "character of the field in which the student is to work."[20] Here

Harper sought to base the curriculum on the external environment that influenced the minister and his parishioners. His main concern was with the democratic form of government that pervaded America yet confounded the typical churchperson who was accustomed to the aristocratic attitude of the established church. He also stressed, along the same line, the need for the curriculum to be in touch with the lower classes of society. The minister had to receive a training that would prepare him to "think," to "adapt to his environment," and to "be of practical service."

The curriculum changes, if adopted, were to alter significantly the profession of the ministry. In another essay titled "Why Are There Fewer Students for the Ministry?" Harper outlined his reasons for the 15 percent decline of students enrolled in northern Protestant seminaries between 1884 and 1904.[21] The reasons were clearly related to his previously stated criticisms of theological education generally, namely, people did not want to enter a profession that was archaic, narrow-minded, and unscientific. Such a set of conditions had led to the loss of esteem and respect for the ministry as a profession. The minister's standing had fallen in the eyes of the younger generation and the brightest students were seeking careers in law, medicine, or business. The seminaries aided the decline by admitting and graduating the untrained. The minister was "no longer the one person in the community who stands high above the others, and, for that reason, if no other, commands the esteem and respect of all."[22]

One might assume from Harper's commitment to modern scientific methods that the new divinity school at Chicago would have had a strong research orientation. Surprisingly, in the bulletin authored by Harper early in his presidency that outlined his vision for the divinity school, there was no mention of a scientific or scholarly purpose.[23] In *Official Bulletin No. 5* Harper took up the issue of the role and purpose of the divinity school:

> *Its Purpose*: the purpose of the Seminary is primarily and chiefly to fit men to become preachers of the Gospel. To this end students are instructed in the great doctrines of the Bible, in the chief facts and teachings of Church History, in the critical translation and interpretation of the Old and New Testaments, in the constitution and management of churches, in the composition and delivery of sermons, and in the practical duties of the pastorate.[24]

The primary focus of the school was to be the training of minsters and Christian workers. Harper sought to elevate the educational standards of his enterprise by requiring a bachelor of arts degree of all students who received the bachelor of divinity. The academic structure would consist of eight departments: (1) Old Testament literature and exegesis, (2) New Testament literature and exegesis, (3) biblical theology, (4) apologetics, (5) systematic theology, (6) church history, (7) the homiletics, ecclesiastical polity, and pastoral duties department, and (6) missions and missions work. In keeping with Harper's interest in the practical side of religious education, students were required to engage in some form of field religious work, e.g., city mission volunteer or Sunday school teacher.

The fact that Harper's original academic scheme for the divinity school did not include a specific research provision does not signify an antiscientific bias in regard to the study of religious and biblical topics. Despite the practical and ministerial purpose of the divinity school, Harper increasingly came to recognize the research function of the seminary. This realization is most easily discovered in looking through Harper's annual reports as they refer to the work of the seminary. Although *Official Bulletin No. 5* did not specifically mention research, in the decennial president's report Harper spoke to the tension between the scholarly and the practical purposes of the divinity school:

> the line between scientific Divinity, if such a phrase may be used, and practical Divinity must be more sharply drawn, and such reorganization of the work should be brought about as will adapt it more closely to the needs of different classes of students.[25]

If Harper's realization of the importance of research in religion in the divinity school gradually evolved, he was, nevertheless, from the founding of the university in 1892 aware of the need for academic religion study unfettered by practical ministerial work. As part of the agreement for the transfer of the Baptist Theological Union to the University of Chicago as its divinity school, it was stipulated that "instruction in the Old Testament and Semitic department shall be provided by the University; that is the instructors of this department shall be members of the Faculty of the Graduate School."[26] Harper was the chairman of the Semitic department and guided its growth. Although Harper never made a specific statement as to why the Semitic department was placed in the graduate school and not the divinity school, one may safely assume that he was carrying on the practice he had at Yale where the Ph.D. was awarded for Semitics through the university since the divinity school offered only bachelor's degrees. Most important, however, Harper made one other decisive move to place religious research on scholarly ground—in

1892 the university opened with a Department of Comparative Religion under the auspices of the faculty of arts, science, and literature.

C. Comparative Religion

William Rainey Harper was well aware of advances made in comparative religion in the latter part of the nineteenth century. His own acceptance of the critical methods of biblical interpretation and his interest in the history of the Hebrew nation paved the way for a keen appreciation for the proper role of the comparison of world religions. In his own scholarship he compared the rites and rituals of the Israelites with those of her neighbors. Such comparisons often led him to postulate that the Hebrews borrowed many of their religious names and practices from neighboring peoples. The biblical accounts of the Fall of Man and the Great Flood, for example, were not unique to Israel; they were not "literal history."

There was, for Harper, nevertheless, a superiority and distinctiveness to the Judeao-Christian tradition. In comparing the Great Flood as it appears in the biblical account with other literature he concluded:

> The deluge was a fact; it was a part of a great plan; its record as handed down to us in the Hebrew Scriptures is the one clear, distinct account, and when compared with the other accounts bears on its face indications of its divine origin.[27]

This respect for other religions yet persistent belief in the distinctiveness of Judaism and Christianity became focused in Harper's analysis of the World's Parliament of Religions. At the time the parliament was holding its final sessions, Harper commented on its significance in an editorial in *The Biblical World*.[28] He openly acknowledged that other religions were not "false" in contradistinction to the "true" gospel. God was at work in all of the religions of humankind and to dismiss religious traditions and their practitioners as pagans was to fail to realize that they were "from God."[29]

Nevertheless, Harper resolutely clung to the all-encompassing nature and uniqueness of Christianity. It was, he argued, under the auspices of the Christian Church, in a Christian land, that the parliament was held. The comparative study of religion was a "science born in Christian lands" and the profoundest concern for the religious spirit was instrumental in bringing about the comparison of Christianity with other religions. Most important, the parliament illustrated the centrality of the spirit of Christ. Much more important than the theological systems surrounding Christianity, the person of Christ was discovered to be the ground of all religion:

> The ultimate religion, from the platform of the Parliament of Religions, is seen to be that one which has the greatest capacity of growth manward and Godward. It need not be said that the Christ of Christianity is not only the centre but the boundless circumference of religion. For man ultimateness must be in a living person. In this sense not Christianity but Christ is the ultimate religion. Such was the deepest voice of this Parliament.[30]

Harper's interest in world religions, heightened by the Parliament of Religions, was not limited to abstruse arguments or scholarly editorials. It took a very practical form when Harper in 1893 began including a special section called "Comparative Religion Notes" in *The Biblical World*. This section presented the latest discoveries concerning comparative religion and served as a rallying point for the new field. It reviewed the latest literature, listed relevant academic appointments in America and Europe, and occasionally charted the uncertain waters of the discipline. Alternately expressing hope that the nascent field of knowledge would flourish and concern that not enough official recognition was taking place within higher education, the editors of this section anticipated the next logical step, the creation of a journal of comparative religion. In the August 1896 issue the question was asked, "Is the time come for the establishment of a journal devoted exclusively to this subject, in which those who believe in the future of Comparative Religion may have an opportunity to show their faith by their works?"[31] No such journal was established.

Some of Harper's earliest knowledge of the blossoming discipline of comparative religion came from his long-time friend George S. Goodspeed. Goodspeed had been corresponding with Harper from Germany, where the former had gone to study in 1891. On December 13, 1891 Goodspeed wrote to Harper from Freiburg, "I am all on fire in my interest in Comp. Religion and Anc. History. It is *the* field—beyond comparison. Everything contributes to it; everything is subsidiary to it."[32]

Goodspeed's excitement about the discipline gave Harper an opportunity to make an original contribution to higher education and the academic study of religion. Instead of locating the study of comparative religion in the divinity school, Harper placed the Department of Comparative Religion under the faculties of arts, literature, and science of the university. Chicago's annual register for 1893-94 listed George S. Goodspeed as associate professor of comparative religion and John Barrows, the Chicago Presbyterian minister made famous by his leadership of the Parliament of Religions at the Columbian Exposition in 1893, as professorial lecturer in comparative religion. Four courses of instruction were offered that year. Although there was a close relationship with the divinity school, Harper's new Department of Comparative Religion had distinct course offerings, its own fellowships, and offered a doctor's degree.

Harper's concern for the standing and importance of religion in his new educational enterprise was complete. The university as a whole had a religious purpose as the new Messiah, the mediator of knowledge. The divinity school was to train religious workers. And finally, the new scientific methods were to have a home in the university not only in the Semitic department, but also in the Department of Comparative Religion. A graduate school for the investigation of religious questions, unhampered by ecclesiastical stringencies or professional concerns, was a reality. Scholars would pursue a research agenda and train future scholars in the blossoming Religionswissenschaft. John Barrows echoed the sentiments of Harper when he expressed optimistically soon after the Department of Comparative Religion opened:

> This department will, I hope, inspire in the generations of scholars who are to pass through these halls, the joy of discovering the treasures of truth which are hidden, with much of rubbish and error, in the sacred books of the world.[33]

Religion, both for the scholar and the potential minister, would play a central role in Harper's university. Harper had set in place the first nonsectarian, graduate research program in religious studies in America.

Charles W. Eliot

Charles Eliot's role in raising turn-of-the-century Harvard University out of relative mediocrity into full-blown educational prominence is well documented.[34] Inaugurated as president in 1869, Eliot orchestrated Harvard's metamorphosis at a time when the American university was rising like a phoenix from the ashes of the antebellum college. Eliot became one of the best-known educators in America and was a highly respected speaker and author long after his resignation in 1909 from the Harvard presidency.

Much less familiar, however, was the religious dimension of the man who led Harvard for four decades and how those religious beliefs may have influenced his leadership. In no small part this was due to Eliot's extreme reserve in personal matters, even among his closest friends. In a May 19, 1894, letter to Harvard faculty member George H. Palmer, Eliot confided, "I am by nature reserved except with intimates, and even with some of them." The letter went on to say that he was happy, therefore, that Palmer, not an intimate, had been able to detect his reliance on the Almighty for sustenance.

> It has been hard to have people suppose—even some of my friends—that my interest in the religious policy of the university was a matter of expediency and not of conviction. I am glad that you have inferred from my habitual conduct an underlying conviction.[35]

Eliot's underlying convictions had their origin in the liberal tradition of the New England Congregationalism of his Boston upbringing. His father was warden and choirmaster at King's Chapel, a church in Boston recognized for its leadership in the movement for liberal religion in the revolt against extreme Calvinism. Eliot became a Sunday school teacher at King's Chapel and was early in his life influenced by the movement that took, in 1825, the name Unitarian.[36]

The religion of Eliot's family, which accompanied him throughout his life, was foremost a belief in the goodness of humanity. The essential worth of humankind, the rejection of dogma, and the immanence of God's presence in persons and nature were the cornerstones around which he built his personal faith. He often acknowledged his debt to two great liberal New Englanders, William Ellery Channing and Ralph Waldo Emerson, for clarifying and giving direction to his thought.[37]

Above all, religion for Eliot was a disposition, an attitude. One did not need to rely on the organized church to interpret God's will or direct one's life. God was not to be "discovered" because "in Him we live and move and have our being, literally, completely, and now."[38] Religion encompassed the beautiful and truthful in each human being. God spoke through the spirit of each individual, not occasionally or supernaturally, but naturally. People were inevitably religious beings and could not achieve their best without giving expression to their religious spirits. In a speech in 1914 addressing the need for a renewed Christianity, Eliot said succinctly, "After all, true Christianity is not a body of doctrines, or an official organization to direct and control men's minds and wills. *It is a way of life.*"[39]

In 1909 Eliot presented his most famous and controversial statement on religion, in an address given before the Harvard Summer School of Theology entitled "The Religion of the Future."[40] Condemned by much of the religious and secular press as heterodox or heretical, the speech outlined the characteristics which would increasingly embody the religion of the twentieth century.[41] Denying any need for authority in religion, either temporal or spiritual, Eliot spoke of the immanence of God and the centrality such immanence would play in the religion of the future. The new religion was to be grounded in "a humane and worthy idea of God, thoroughly consistent with the nineteenth century revelations concerning man and nature." God is "so absolutely immanent in all things, animate and inanimate, that no mediation is needed between him and the least particle of his creation."[42]

The emphasis on God's immanence led Eliot naturally to the dignity of the human soul and love for humankind. The positive and fruitful things of life were to form the core of daily religious practice. The new religion was to be an "all-saints religion." Evil was to be approached from an attitude of resistance, not as a necessary condition of human nature. Love, hope, truth, and beauty were to be the dogma of the new church. The unity of God and humanity and the fellowship of humankind were to crown the new religion. Eliot stated:

> The new religion will make but slow progress so far as outward organization goes. It will, however, progressively modify the creeds and religious practices of all the existing churches, and change their symbolism and their teachings concerning the conduct of life. Since its chief doctrine is the doctrine of a sublime unity of substance, force, and spirit, and its chief precept is, Be Serviceable, it will exert a strong unifying influence among men.[43]

A. Science, Religion, and the University

Eliot's personal religious faith opened him up to the intellectual methods and discoveries that permeated his late-nineteenth-century world. The dignity of individuals and immanence of God meant no retreat from the forces of science and a hearty acceptance of the humanistic movements of society. Eliot's

53

own education was concentrated in the areas of chemistry and mathematics and he took from those early years a love and commitment to science and investigation. In his 1877-78 president's annual report, he said, "for the modern world respects only the scientific method, which admits of no settled convictions except those which rest upon thorough previous investigation."[44]

The scientific method became, for Eliot, the sine qua non of the educational world. Inextricably linked to knowledge and progress, science was the new master of the modern spirit. Furthermore, the scientific method was not an obstacle to religion but rather an accomplice in the search for truth and pure knowledge. When utilized correctly, science could correct erroneous dogmas and archaic practices that deadened organized religion. Eliot often punctured his speeches with examples of how science triumphed where religion erred.[45] By denying, ignoring, or attempting to disparage the scientific method, religion was in complete contradiction to the spirit of the times and the essence of its own nature. When God and humanity and nature were one, science and religion were cojoined. Eliot stated simply in a manuscript entitled "The Place of Religion in a College," "there is no separating God from nature, or religion from science, or things sacred from things secular."[46]

Religion, then, was to be in harmony with the great secular movements of society (e.g., democracy, individualism, and social idealism) and the spirit of research that was to characterize the university. The near-pantheism of Eliot's theology linked science and religion. The scientific standards that ruled the university community were not antireligious but rather coterminous with religion. By doing its work in its own way the university was to fulfill a religious purpose.

Although he never spoke at length on the religious purpose of higher education, at two presidential inaugural ceremonies Eliot conveyed his underlying belief in the spiritual mission of the university. The first was his own inaugural address delivered on October 19, 1869. In his speech Eliot demonstrated a remarkable grasp of the range of responsibilities, challenges, and tasks confronting Harvard College and higher education at that time. Central to his thinking, however, was the need for investigation and the openness of mind that such investigation breeds in the university. Intellectual freedom was the watchword of academic life. A true university could not be built by a sect; the religious purpose of the educational world was found in unfettered methods of research.

The worthy fruit of academic culture is an open mind, trained to careful thinking, instructed in the methods of philosophic investigation, acquainted in a general way with the accumulated thought of past generations, and penetrated with humility. *It is thus that the university in our day serves Christ and the church.*[47]

Seven years later Eliot again took the opportunity to equate the work of the university with a spiritual purpose. Speaking at the inauguration of Daniel C. Gilman as first president of Johns Hopkins University on February 22, 1876, Eliot answered critics who claimed a nondenominational university would be irreligious:

It would be a fearful portent if thorough study of nature and of man in all his attributes and works, such as befits a university, led scholars to impiety. But it does not; on the contrary, such study fills men with humility and awe, by bringing them on every hand face to face with inscrutable mystery and infinite power. The whole work of a university is uplifting, refining, and spiritualizing; it embraces "Whatsoever touches life with upward impulse; be He nowhere else, God is in all that liberates and lifts. In all that humbles, sweetens, and consoles."[48]

With the university so intimately connected with the truth that forms the basis of religion, Eliot went the next logical step by proclaiming that a non-denominational institution of higher learning provided the best training for ministers. The archaic, dogmatic, and unscientific approach that typified the nineteenth-century denominational seminary was anathema to Eliot. The new university was best suited to fit modern ministers for their profession, a profession which, according to Eliot, had changed greatly. Influenced by the broad societal changes around them, modern ministers derived their authority from the strength of their character, the depth of their intelligence, and the breadth of their learning. Such traits were cultivated in the academic context of a university or its affiliated seminary.

Eliot's proposal to make university training appropriate for the profession of the ministry found expression in "On the Education of Ministers," published originally in May 1883 in *The Princeton Review*.[49] After reviewing the changes which had transformed society and how they affected the ministry, Eliot underscored the fundamental revolution that radically altered the ministerial profession and opened the clergy to university instruction. The basic transformation was the new standard of research, the scientific method of impartial investigation, which encompassed both layman and minister. The

55

growth of the physical and natural sciences and the corresponding acceptance of the scientific method "has set up a new standard of intellectual sincerity, and Protestant theologians and ministers must rise to that standard, if they would continue to command the respect of mankind."[50]

The arrival of this new standard meant a change in the theological education that prepared young ministers for their role in society. Dogmatic teachings and sectarian teachers had no place. The professor had to have the freedom of judgment commanded by the scientific method. This freedom was assured in universities:

> It simply means that the teacher is free to think and say whatever seems to him good, and to change his mind as often as he likes; and that the pupil is free to adopt whatever opinions or theories most commend themselves to his judgment after he has studied the subject. This academic freedom is much more likely to be obtained in the universities, and in cities which are large enough to be centers of diversified intellectual activity, than it is in isolated denominational seminaries.[51]

Eliot's view of the proper role and mission of the university thus reached into the very heart of religion, the training of the clergy. Intimately connected to his personal Unitarian religious beliefs and centered in his unyielding faith in science and the investigative method, religion was to be no stranger in his educational world. There remained only one more puzzle piece to put into place, a separate structure to house religious studies.

B. Harvard Divinity School

The Harvard Divinity School had a history that long preceded the arrival of Charles W. Eliot in 1869. When Eliot became president, however, it did not take him long to decry the weakness of the seminary. In his annual report of 1874-75 he bluntly stated,

> The condition of the [Divinity] School is to be deeply regretted, for the sake of both the public and of the University. . . . To remedy the feebleness of the School seems to be beyond the power of its learned and devoted Faculty, of the Governing Boards, and of the Administrator of the University.[52]

Eliot chose to lift the divinity school to a place of equality with the other departments and divisions of the university. In this endeavor he faced no small task. The traditions of low admittance standards and changing degree requirements were hard to rectify. In the first half of the nineteenth century a young man was admitted to the divinity school with little educational preparation and a note confirming his upright moral character. By simply making a request, three or more years after graduation, an alumnus would receive a master's degree. And, a tradition that Eliot condemned openly and frequently, divinity school students paid much less in tuition and fees than other students.[53]

These problems Eliot gradually corrected. The faculty and student body came to be recognized for their scholarly activity and took their place alongside the rest of the university community. Hugh Hawkins was correct when he stated, "By keeping theology in the university as a respected intellectual discipline, Harvard Divinity School in Eliot's day made its greatest contribution."[54]

Eliot's plan for the divinity school differed very little from what he had in mind for the university as a whole. Although Unitarian in its origin, the divinity school was to remain nondenominational. No particular religious allegiance was required either of faculty or students. Eliot reiterated in his 1878-79 annual report,

> A student of theology may enter the [divinity] school, receive its scholarships if he need and deserve pecuniary aid, and win its honors, without an inquiry being made as to what he believes or does not believe, or as to what religious organization he belongs to or proposes to join. Greater freedom cannot be secured.[55]

Eliot's concern that the school remain nonsectarian was evident in his selection of faculty. Always mindful of Harvard's Unitarian heritage, Eliot nevertheless often reminded his audiences of the diversity of denominations represented on the Harvard Divinity School faculty. The facts substantiate Eliot's claim. In 1880 Crawford Howell Toy, a Baptist, was appointed as Hancock Professor of Hebrew and Oriental Languages and in 1882 David Gordon Lyon, another Baptist, was appointed as Hollis Professor of Divinity. Eliot was able to observe this gradual transformation to diversity and in his 1900-1901 annual report, referring to the tenure of divinity school dean Charles Carroll Everett between 1878 and 1900, he claimed Everett had seen the divinity school, which had been almost exclusively Unitarian, "become the resort of students of many different denominations."[56]

Eliot's second major objective was to make the divinity school as committed to the methods of science as any other part of the university. The divinity school faculty did, in fact, raise the level of scholarship to the point that their reputation became widespread. Eliot often argued for the scientific treatment of theological subjects and his argument was usually in response to criticism levied against the divinity school.

There were essentially two criticisms made of Harvard Divinity School as it became more scientific and nondenominational. The first was that it was improper to train ministers of any sort in a university. The second was that it was impossible to teach Christian theology in a nonsectarian, research-oriented institution. Eliot chose his annual report of 1878-79 to answer directly these criticisms and state anew the university's position regarding theological learning.

The first issue Eliot answered by reference to a Supreme Court decision in 1855. In 1852 the Harvard Corporation and Overseers applied to the Supreme Court to be relieved from the responsibility of administering trusts and other endowments given to support theological education. The corporation's desire was to establish a separate divinity school administered by an independent board of trustees. The court denied the request and dismissed the bill on grounds that it would threaten the "perpetuity and sacredness of all our great public charities." The result of this decision, Eliot argued, was to lay the responsibility for theological education, especially that specifically provided for in trusts, directly in the hands of Harvard College and Divinity School.

Of more importance, however, than Harvard's legal responsibility was Eliot's personal motivation for the appropriateness of theological studies in higher education. He believed science had shaken the foundations of learning and was applicable to all subjects, religion included. The humanities were in this sense no different from the natural sciences, for all were matters of pure science and appropriate for the scientific method. Religion was not appropriate only for ministers, but for the undergraduate as well. Eliot provided a fascinating defense of the need for theological studies in the university:

> . . . it is important to observe that, as regards the appropriateness to university instruction of the subjects ordinarily, though inaccurately, designated as theological, the grounds for any difference of opinion whatever among men of learning are very narrow. These subjects are by common consent as liberal and as unsectarian as chemistry, philosophy, or history, with the exception of Christian dogmatic theology, which is quantitatively a very small proportion of

their enormous mass. Thus, Hebrew, Arabic, and other Oriental languages, ecclesiastical history, the literature and criticism of the New Testament, ethics, natural theology, philosophy in its relation to religion, ethnic religions, and the history of religions are all, when properly defined and treated, matters of pure science, which, in every university worthy of the name, should be studied not only by persons who expect to make a professional use of them, but also by young men, graduates or undergraduates, who pursue them as elements of liberal culture. The expediency of grouping the professorships which deal with these subjects into a separate organization called a Divinity School may, perhaps, be reasonably questioned, either now or hereafter, as it has been repeatedly in the past; but it cannot be doubted that the subjects themselves possess an exalted and enduring intellectual interest which make them necessary parts of a comprehensive scheme of university instruction.[57]

Many of the Religionswissenschaft scholars of the late nineteenth and early twentieth centuries would have applauded the above defense of religious studies. Perhaps more than any other university president of his time, Eliot championed a thoroughly scientific treatment of religion. As I note in the next chapter, the history of religions had a long tradition at Harvard as part of the standard curriculum in the divinity school and with the arrival of George Foot Moore in 1902 it was given departmental status. Moreover, Eliot's elective system opened theological studies to nondivinity students. In 1893, a year after William Rainey Harper initiated a graduate program in comparative religion at the University of Chicago, Eliot wrote in his annual report:

Among the many changes which the present century has wrought in the constitution of society and of the University, are, first, the separation of theological education from preliminary training in the liberal arts, and secondly and later the adoption of theological studies as themselves liberal arts.[58]

Charles Eliot's Unitarian theology provided the foundation from which he could give religious studies equal standing with other subjects in the curriculum. William Rainey Harper, on the other hand, derived a religious purpose for the university from a scripturally based messianic vision. The outcome, in both cases, was a welcoming of Religionswissenschaft. For both men the university was the proper place to study religion and to study it—Christian theology included—scientifically. Moreover, the scientific study of religion was appropriate for minister and scholar alike.

THREE

Students of the Science of Religion

The success of the research university at the turn of the century, Harvard and Chicago included, was due in large part to the tremendous number of students matriculating in the colleges, graduate divisions, and professional schools of the new educational enterprises. Total undergraduate enrollment between 1870 and 1890 almost tripled, and by 1909 six American universities had enrollments of more than five thousand students.[1] At Harvard the total enrollment between 1890 and 1920 increased from 2,550 to 7,445 students. At the University of Chicago, the total number of students grew from 594 in the autumn of 1892 to 5,955 in the autumn of 1920.

The decline in the number of divinity students during these years stands in stark contrast to the general growth. The dwindling student matriculation in divinity schools nationwide was wellknown to educators at the time.[2] Harvard Divinity School and the Divinity School of the University of Chicago were no exception as Chicago enrolled 328 students in the divinity school in the autumn of 1892 and only 119 in the fall of 1920. Harvard's divinity school enrollment between the fall of 1890 and the fall of 1920 fell from 41 to 17.

The numbers that demonstrate the decline in seminary enrollment tell little about the relationship between students—undergraduate, graduate, and divinity—and the blossoming field of Religionswissenschaft. Were the new programs and courses offered in the history and comparison of world religions popular? What type of student was interested in such a program? Did students perceive that an academic career in religious studies was a possibility? Did any successfully or unsuccessfully seek such a career? The answers to such questions will aid an assessment of the relative strength and influence of Religionswissenschaft at Harvard and Chicago.

The University of Chicago Students

Neither William Rainey Harper nor George Goodspeed was under the illusion that Chicago's new Department of Comparative Religion would attract great numbers of students. The nascent discipline had European origins and much of the relevant research and scholarship took place across the ocean from North America. When the University of Chicago opened in 1892, only the vaguest outlines of Religionswissenschaft were known to the average American student who may have had an interest in religion.

George S. Goodspeed was explicit about his fear of being unable to attract students to his new program. In an April 14, 1892 letter to Harper from Freiburg, Germany, he wrote, "It was not all that evident to me that very much in my line would be taken by students. It is new and must make its way. It has no past of popular favor behind it."[3]

Goodspeed's fears were justified and his prophecy self-fulfilling. The Department of Comparative Religion never enjoyed a strong student enrollment. During the university's first five years, typically one or two instructors (usually George Goodspeed and/or Edmund Buckley) each taught one or two courses per quarter with an average class size of fewer than ten students. The *President's Report of 1897-98* listed twenty-five registrations in comparative religion for the academic year 1892-93 and only eighteen in 1895-97.[4] The small number of registrations in comparative religion meant a very high per-capita cost of instruction. The Department of Comparative Religion from 1894 to 1899 had the greatest increase of any academic department in per-capita cost of instruction—from $49.80 per student to $81.43 per student.[5]

Total class registrations did not usually meet desired levels and the department was unsuccessful in attracting many doctoral candidates. There is no doubt that Goodspeed and Harper both hoped the department would be able to turn out Ph.D.'s in increasing numbers. Although open to all university students, the Department of Comparative Religion was most eager to enroll the potential Religionswissenschaft scholar. Goodspeed often, as the following 1894 memorandum illustrated, pleaded with Harper for the necessary resources to attract mature graduate students who were his foremost concern:

> Our students consist of two classes—first, those who are interested in the subject only in a general way as a help in their more special studies as e.g. students in

divinity—and second, those who desire to make it a special work. These latter are the ones who are especially sought by us and who will do the best service for the department and this special field of learning. But as the subject is at present in its infancy and opportunities for using the knowledge, thus gained, in teaching are appearing very slowly, it is an indispensable necessity for our growth that we have fellowships to attract these special students. The subject is a graduate subject, for mature students of the highest grade, and for them in their research work with us we need scholarships.[6]

Goodspeed was able to attract only a few students to pursue a doctorate in comparative religion. Edmund Buckley received his Ph.D. in 1894 after writing his dissertation on "Japanese Phallicism." Elizabeth Moon followed in 1899 with a thesis entitled "Ideas of Future Life Among the Algonquins," and in 1903 Andrew Fors received his doctorate with a dissertation entitled "The Ethical World-Conception of the Norse People." The comparative religion program was also supported by fellowships. Six fellowships were awarded to three individuals during the first ten years of the department. However, in many of those years the fellowship was simply diverted temporarily from the Semitic department to the Department of Comparative Religion. Moreover, the recipient of the fellowship in comparative religion from 1895 to 1898 was F. J. Coffin, a man who received his Ph.D. in Semitics in 1989 with a dissertation entitled "The Third Commandment."

The relative weakness of the Department of Comparative Religion from the standpoint of attracting doctoral students can best be seen by comparing it with other departments in the Graduate School of Arts and Literature. From the years 1892 to 1902, comparative religion had the fourth lowest total of doctorates awarded among the seventeen departments in the graduate school. The two doctor's degrees earned in comparative religion were far below the total awarded in Semitics (12), Greek (18), history (24), and sociology (23).[7] The situation worsened in the first two decades of the twentieth century and by 1916 the Department of Comparative Religion had awarded just three doctorates, the lowest of any of the then twenty departments that made up the Graduate School of Arts and Literature.[8]

Although the number of potential Religionswissenschaft scholars was small, the question remains as to their potential for academic appointment, publishing opportunities, and their own sense of professional identity. What did a Ph.D. in comparative religion signify, personally and professionally, for the young scholar at the turn of the century? Perhaps the best way to answer this question is to take a brief look at the careers of two individuals, Chicago's Edmund Buckley and Elizabeth Moon.

The story of Edmund Buckley's life is a sketchy one derived from a few scattered sources.[9] He was born in Birmingham, England, in 1855 and traveled to America where he matriculated at the University of Michigan in 1881. At Michigan he received his A.B. and A.M. degrees in 1884; the latter degree was awarded from the Department of Literature. From Michigan he went to Europe and studied privately in Berlin (1884-85) and London (1885-86). Presumably gaining an interest in philosophical and theological subjects, Buckley taught from 1886 to 1892 for the American Board of Missions at Doshisba College in Kyoto, Japan, as professor of theistic philosophy.

Travel through China, India, Egypt, and Palestine followed before Buckley received the Rabbi Hirsch Fellowship in Comparative Religion at the University of Chicago for the academic year 1893-94. Taking only a year to finish his doctorate, he so impressed George S. Goodspeed that one month after his graduation Goodspeed recommended Buckley to President Harper "as Docent in the department of Comp. Religion beginning Jan. 1st, 1895."[10]

Harper concurred with Goodspeed and from 1895 to 1899 Buckley, as docent, taught many courses in comparative religion, usually specializing in Eastern religions or the science of religion. From 1899 to 1907 he limited himself to teaching during the summer quarter, sporadically offering courses on the history of religions or the science of religion. Although the reasons for his separation from the University of Chicago are not clear, Buckley's docentship in comparative religion became, in his own words in 1910, merely a "sinecure."

Buckley had a fair amount of success publishing articles in Religionswissenschaft during his years at Chicago and immediately thereafter. In 1897 the highly regarded *Lehrbuch der Religionsgeschichte*, edited by Chantepie de la Saussaye, carried his articles on Chinese, Japanese, and Mongol religions.[11] Eighteen ninety-seven was also the year in which *Universal Religion* was published, a voluminous history of religion that Buckley both edited and contributed articles to.[12] *The Biblical World* carried a number of his articles and book reviews.[13] Buckley was also often called on to lecture, usually on the topic of Eastern religions.

A Congregationalist with a liberal persuasion, Buckley did not find it easy to pursue a career as a lecturer, author, and teacher in comparative religion. In May 1900, he was asked by George Goodspeed to return to campus to conduct a tour of the Haskell Museum of Comparative Religion and to give a lecture. Buckley agreed and went on to explain to Goodspeed that he was in Michigan "making the bread and butter that hierology has failed to supply, by organizing classes for the study of the social sciences." He concluded his letter, "I seem destined to wander topically as well as topographically."[14]

Buckley's wanderings finally took him to Kramer, Indiana, as a lecturer on ethnology, art, and religion at the Mudlavia Sanitarium from 1908 to 1920.[15] He ceased to publish and seemed unable to find an academic context that would enable him to carry forward his Religionswissenschaft research interests. Finally, in December 1918, he turned to his alma mater in Chicago in an attempt to secure an academic appointment. He wrote a lengthy letter to President Judson, reviewing his professional record in religious studies and offering himself as a candidate for the professorship of comparative religion. The courses he proposed to teach included the history of religions; the science of religion; Japanese, Chinese, and Indian religions; and the philosophy of religion. He claimed he was "the only person in America available as an instructor in comparative religion (hierology or history and science of religion) who could use both his own text-book and his own collection" and offered that he could "commence instruction on a few days notice at any time."[16] In view of the fact that the mainstay of the Department of Comparative Religion at the time, George Burman Foster, died just six days after Buckley penned his letter, it is interesting that Buckley was not offered the position he sought.

Edmund Buckley's inability to secure an academic career in comparative religion in part reflects the lack of a blossoming academic environment for Religionswissenschaft. Academic opportunities were almost nonexistent and Buckley was destined to peddle his course offering in religion in an ad hoc manner. In 1920 he became professor of psychology at the John Marshall Law School in Chicago, where he taught liberal arts courses to students in preparatory classes. In 1927 he retired to St. Petersburg, Florida, and on February 28, 1934, after a brief illness, he died.

It is very likely that Edmund Buckley, when he was a docent at the University of Chicago, was acquainted with Elizabeth Laetitia Moon. Moon received her doctorate in comparative religion from Chicago in 1899. She had earlier graduated from Smith College with an A.B. degree (1894) and an M.A. degree (1896). Her interest in religion was evident in her thesis topic, "Attitudes of Religions to One Another."

During the academic year 1897-98, Moon studied at the Sorbonne in Paris. There she attended the lectures of M. Leon Marillier, professor of the religion of uncivilized peoples at the Ecole des Hautes Etudes and joint editor with

Jean Reville of the *Revue de l'histoire des religions*. It was under Marillier that Moon gained an interest in the history of religions. After Marillier's premature death in 1902, Moon wrote his obituary for *The Open Court*.

> It was my privilege to attend his lectures and work under his direction during the year 1897-1898. The two subjects discussed were Marriage Rites and Human Sacrifices among uncivilized peoples. . . . He was remarkable in combining the characteristics of specialist and philosopher. While making thorough studies on such lines as sacrifices or ideas of the future life among uncivilized peoples he had a broad comprehension of the whole field of religion.[17]

Moon carried her interest in the religion and culture of uncivilized peoples with her to Chicago, where she wrote her dissertation on the topic of the ideas of the future life among the Algonquin Indians. She remained fascinated with the history and rituals of the American Indians in the years immediately following her Chicago graduation, and in the summer of 1902 she visited the Quinault Indians in the state of Washington, a visit that led to the publication of an article in *The Open Court*.[18]

Her marriage in 1900 to Henry Conard ultimately resulted in 1906 in a move to Grinnell, Iowa, where Conard had taken a professorship of botany at Grinnell College. The raising of four children occupied most of her time during the second and third decades of the twentieth century but she took an active role in social, religious, and political movements of the time. Of Quaker heritage, she remained a pacifist throughout her life and authored many articles on the subject of peace in the Quaker publication *The Friend*. In 1920 she cofounded the Grinnell, Iowa, chapter of the League of Women Voters and in 1932 she was a candidate for the governor of Iowa on the Socialist Party ticket.[19]

In addition to crusading for many social causes, Moon remained an active teacher, researcher, and writer until her death in 1946. In 1925 she enrolled in Columbia University in New York for a year of postgraduate study in sociology. Between 1926 and 1941 she taught in the sociology department of Grinnell College, from 1926 to 1937 as lecturer in social economics, and from 1938 to 1941 as a lecturer in sociology. The courses she taught included Social Origins, Social Control, The Family, and Sociology of Urban Life.[20] During these years she also published two articles in the field of sociology.[21]

It is significant that Moon's early interest in the religious life and culture of uncivilized peoples later combined with a broader concern for the sociological issues of family, race, and class. The sociological overtones of her Chicago dissertation were apparent but she also never lost interest in religion. The 1935 Grinnell catalog described her Social Origins course as "a study of the evolution of two institutions: marriage and religion." Sociology provided the professional identity and academic context for Laetitia Moon Conard to carry on her research when comparative religion did not.

If Buckley and Moon had surveyed their fellow classmates at Chicago about their desire for an academic career in religious studies, the results would have been disappointing. In addition to the fact that few teaching or research opportunities were available to the neophyte Religionswissenschafter, Buckley's and Moon's classmates, for the most part, were training for careers in the ministry. Such was the career path of the only other Chicago doctoral graduate in comparative religion, Andrew Peter Fors. He became pastor of the Luther Bethel Church in Chicago before his early death in 1929.

One of the hallmarks of the University of Chicago was the opportunity for students to take courses in other departments or schools of the university. In the senior colleges much flexibility in course selection was allowed and to a great degree students were able to control their own programs.[22] Course requirements at the graduate level were left to the departments and interdisciplinary study was encouraged. In the early years of the Department of Comparative Religion, relevant coursework for the Ph.D. was outlined in annual registers.[23] Indo-European and Semitic religions, the philosophy of religion, and comparative theology were emphasized. Students were encouraged to take advanced coursework in related departments. By 1915 the flexibility of the department, which also, no doubt, reflected its smallness, was evident in the annual register, which stated, "Candidates for degrees in the Department (Comparative Religion) should arrange their work in consultation with the instructor."[24]

The divinity school likewise encouraged its students to select relevant courses in other departments of the university, and many did so. In Harper's *Decennial Report*, divinity school dean Eri Hulbert reported on the registration of divinity students in nondivinity departments between 1893 and 1902. Of the twenty-eight departments listed, eight stand out as significant providers of academic work for divinity students. The eight, in descending order by total number of registrations over the ten-year period, were: sociology (701), literature in English (589), philosophy (327), English (301), public speaking (262), comparative religion (126), Germanic (121), and history (113).[25]

By 1917, however, the Department of Comparative Religion had become the most popular department in the graduate school for seminarians and in that year 116 divinity students took courses in comparative religion.[26] It became increasingly apparent that the divinity school was the chief provider of students for the Department of Comparative Religion, a fact that was acknowledged by Chicago president Harry Pratt Judson:

> The Department of the Semitic Languages and Literature, the Department of Biblical and Patristic Greek, and the Department of Comparative Religion are university departments under the Faculty of Arts, Literature and Science, but offer instruction also to divinity students—and in fact their classes are very largely supplied from the Divinity School.[27]

The University of Chicago's Department of Comparative Religion never realized the dreams of Harper and Goodspeed in terms of becoming a significant training ground for scholars of religion. Its dismal record in the production of doctorates—only three between 1892 and 1920—and the fact that its few courses were primarily populated by divinity students made it an increasingly weak program. By 1923 it was openly regarded as one of the weaker departments in the Graduate School of Arts and Literature.[28]

The Harvard Divinity School Students

Charles W. Eliot's disdain for the anachronistic Christian Church, as noted in the last chapter, did not signify his rejection of the profession of the ministry. The profession had a rightful place within higher education and Eliot welcomed the training of ministers at Harvard. He believed that "to become a serviceable, free, growing minister is a worthy ambition for any intelligent and high-minded young man" and spoke openly of his desire that more Harvard graduates enter the ministry.[29]

It was, then, in the training and preparation of ministers that Harvard Divinity School carried out its fundamental mission. Unlike the University of Chicago's Department of Comparative Religion, the divinity school at Harvard had no expressed intent to teach potential Religionswissenschaft scholars. Whereas controversies occasionally arose over the academic versus the practical value of subjects in the curriculum, such discussions always took place in the context of *theological* education, namely, the context of what value a given subject was to the potential minister. The specific training of scholars of religion was not provided for until the second decade of the twentieth century when the degrees of master of theology and doctor of theology were established (in 1912 and 1914 respectively).

The divinity school's commitment to scientific methods, nevertheless, led to the criticism that the school was becoming too scholarly in orientation. This criticism, which no doubt was also related to increasingly stringent academic requirements for graduation, was of great concern to the overseers of the university. In various committees that the overseers assigned to review the work of the divinity school, the issue of scientific learning versus practical training was often confronted. In 1913, for example, the overseer committee reported:

> The Committee is of the opinion that no reputation for great learning, or for advanced scholarship in the more learned phases of theological education, will compensate for failure to do efficient work in these newer requirements for ministerial training.[30]

In 1934 another committee happily reported that with few exceptions the full-time students at the divinity school were planning to enter the ministry.[31]

Various studies of divinity school alumni were undertaken to counter the growing notion that the school was not fulfilling its role of training ministers. In his 1894-95 annual report, Eliot referred to sixty-four men who graduated from the theological school between 1880 and 1894 who were still living at that time. Of the sixty-four, fifty-five had parishes, one was a professor in a theological school, three never entered the ministry, and one withdrew after entering the ministry.[32] Divinity school dean William W. Fenn followed in 1906-07 with a similar report. He discovered that a ten-year history of graduates of the divinity school (1895-1905) revealed that of forty-nine degree recipients thirty-six were in charge of parishes, three were ordained ministers temporarily without parishes, four were professors in theological seminaries, and two went into business.[33] Equally important, however, was the fact that of the 180 students who attended but did not receive degrees, 114 were in charge of parishes. Fenn summarized the results of his survey:

> This investigation shows, therefore, that students of the School do become parish ministers, and that their distribution among twelve different denominations is what might be expected in the case of a non-denominational school.[34]

The questioning of the divinity school's vocational role and the administration's open attempt to prove the school was, in fact, fulfilling its central ministerial mission raise important questions regarding the student body. What opportunity was there for a Harvard divinity school student at the turn of the century to be exposed to Religionswissenschaft? Did any students seek to become scholars of religion, and did the initiation of the S.T.M. and Th.D. degrees aid in such a search? A look at student classifications and enrollment data will help answer these questions.

The divinity school student at Harvard at the turn of the century carried one of three classifications. Candidates for the degree of bachelor of divinity (S.T.B.) had to have a bachelor of arts degree or an education equal to graduates of "the best New England colleges." Such candidates usually took a three-year course of study. Individuals who had already received a degree from a theological school could be admitted to the divinity school as "Resident Graduates." These students could pursue any course of study approved by the faculty and would, upon request, receive a certificate verifying the student's length of stay and examinations satisfactorily passed. "Special Students" at Harvard Divinity School were those who had received a degree in arts, literature, or science or a fully equivalent education and were non-degree seeking. They likewise could obtain a certificate.

It is revealing to look at the relative proportions of the three types of students at the divinity school between 1890 and 1925. Most important is the fact that the number of S.T.B. degree-seeking students remained fairly stable. In 1890-01, twenty-three students were enrolled in the school as bachelor-degree candidates and in 1925-26 thirty-one students were enrolled.[35] Moreover, the approximate proportion of degree-seeking students was only one-half of the total enrollment throughout these decades. Typically 45 to 55 percent of the students were either resident graduates or special students, with resident graduates usually making up one-third of the student body.[36]

The great numbers of resident graduate and special students and the financial burdens confronting many S.T.B. students led to an enormous attrition problem at the divinity school. President Eliot spoke to this problem in his annual report of 1891-92 when he commented that of the forty divinity school students enrolled in 1891-92 only fifteen had re-enrolled in 1892-93.[37] Levering Reynolds, Jr., in an essay about the divinity school's history between 1880 and 1953, reported that the percentage of students leaving the school without degrees from 1880 to 1907 averaged almost 75 percent.[38] The high attrition rates indicate the difficulty Harvard Divinity School had in attracting mature, full-time students who would be more likely to pursue an academic career in religious studies.

Charles C. Everett, dean from 1878 to 1900, was very aware of the attrition problem at Harvard, especially among graduate students. The following quotes, taken from his 1890-91 and 1894-95 annual reports, illustrate the role Harvard had in providing an elective, short-term education to ministers who had no intention of pursuing a career of scholarship:

> The figures that have been given show that teaching the graduates forms an increasing element in the work of the School and make it evident how imperfectly this work is represented by the number of the Graduating Class. While this class numbered only six, twenty-nine men, who had been under the instruction of the School taking complete or partial courses for a whole or part of the year, left during the year, twenty-four of them at the end of the year. Two of these left with the purpose of returning and completing their course. The fact that so many enter, intending to remain only a year or two, necessarily changes somewhat the character of the School. A large proportion of the men are new every year. The elective system makes it easy for a man to remain a year or two, selecting what seems to him most important, and then to leave, going perhaps to another school, or seeking some field of labor. The habit of dividing one's professional studies among different universities, taking what is most special in each, as is often done in Germany, is perhaps not a bad one. So far as this School is concerned, this method of study enables it to meet and to influence more persons than was formerly possible, while there is no falling in the number of those who take the three-year's course. There is thus gain with no loss in the present condition of affairs.[39]

> So far as the relation of the School to other departments of the University is concerned, they [enrollment data] show that the graduate students enrolled in it [Divinity School] were where they properly belonged; that is, that they were actually preparing for the ministry. So far as certain outside criticisms are concerned, they show that the School does not educate merely theologians and publishers as such, but that it has been very successful in the training of working ministers.[40]

The students who attended Harvard Divinity School as either resident graduates or special students were usually ministers seeking additional coursework. Serious candidates for Religionswissenschaft were rare. What occasionally happened, however, was that a minister became excited about the history of religions or comparative religion through his exposure to Religionswissenschaft as a resident graduate student. The Reverend Franklin N. Riale was such a student.

As Pastor of the East Side Presbyterian Church in Cleveland, Ohio, in 1886, Franklin Riale took a one-year leave of absence to study at Harvard Divinity School. Registered as a resident graduate during the academic year 1887-88, Riale developed a keen interest in comparative religion, which later led to his publishing a number of articles in the discipline.[41] In November 1896, he wrote to President Eliot to express displeasure that Eliot had not written a letter of recommendation to the U.S. commissioner of education for Riale's proposed study on "The Higher Educational Work of the New South." In his letter to Eliot, Riale reviewed his days at Harvard:

> Out of my Harvard work has grown the deepest interest in Comparative Religion—as a "middle-man" of course, and not as an original investigator or specialist. My articles along this line in the *Popular Science Monthly*, *Biblical World*, *Arena*, and other periodicals have been most kindly received and widely quoted in the "Public Opinion" and elsewhere. . . . Dr. Barrows, Chairman of the Parliament of Religions, of his own accord wrote me in the highest praise of my published work.[42]

Franklin Riale's self-designation as a middleman in comparative religion was decidedly accurate. His published works in the new discipline revealed a remarkable familiarity with the methods and discoveries affecting the neophyte field yet he remained committed to the ministry as a vocation.[43] His experience illustrates a pattern not atypical of the Harvard Divinity School student who took an interest in Religionswissenschaft under the tutelage of one of the great scholars on Harvard's faculty. A minister, missionary, or recent seminary graduate entered the divinity school as a resident graduate or special student and was exposed to the history of religions or comparative religion. That exposure translated into a lifelong interest in Religionswissenschaft through reading and occasionally publishing while pursuing the career of pastor or missionary.

This pattern did not signify, however, an absence of opportunity to conduct degree-related graduate study in the history and comparison of world religions. With the arrival of George Foot Moore in 1902, the history of religions was designated a subdivision under the division of history in arts and sciences. Moore worked closely with other arts and sciences faculty to round out a small program in the history of religions. Nevertheless, the program was offered only as a minor field of study and few students took advantage of it. Of the 349 resident graduate students in 1904-05, 2 took partial work in the history of religions. The following year only 3 of 378 resident graduate students did some specialized work in the history of religions. These few students were typically registered as graduate students in Semitic languages, history, or philosophy and were studying the history of religions as a secondary field. If college teaching was their goal after graduation, they would most likely have been hired in their primary fields of concentration.

Any opportunity for George Foot Moore's program in the history of religions to become a unit of the Graduate School of Arts and Sciences ceased when the divinity school decided to offer its own master's and doctor's degrees. Although Moore worked with a few arts and sciences graduate students during his initial years at Harvard, after 1910 no graduate student did even partial study in the history of religions. This was due in large part to the divinity school's initiation of the S.T.M. degree in 1912 and the Th.D. in 1914. The Th.D. was offered in three areas, the Old and New Testaments, the history of Christianity, and Christian theology. As a subfield under Christian theology, the history and philosophy of religion was offered for the Th.D. student.

It thus became possible for a graduate student in the divinity school to work with George Foot Moore and receive a Th.D. in the special field of the history and philosophy of religion under the general field of theology. The Th.D. was designed for serious scholars who sought teaching careers in theological schools. Despite the increasing popularity of the Th.D. and S.T.M. for Harvard divinity students—thirty-eight S.T.M.'s and fourteen Th.D.'s were given out between 1915 and 1925—few chose to specialize in the emerging discipline of the history of religion.

Specifically, three divinity students did a significant portion of their work with George Foot Moore in the special field of the history and philosophy of religion and received the Th.D. Charles Lynn Pyatt received his doctorate in 1916 with his thesis "Moral Teachings of the Jews at the Time of Christ." Carl Friedrich Pfatteicher wrote his dissertation on "The Development of the Conception of God in German Protestant Hymnody" and was awarded his degree in 1922. Finally, Peter Brunner, a student from Germany, received a Th.D. in 1927 after writing his thesis "Probleme der Theleologie bei Maimonides, Thomas von Aquin und Spinoza."[44] In addition, three divinity students received the S.T.M. under Moore in the history of religions: James Thayer Addison in 1917, Max Hugo Vatter in 1921, and Leopold H. R. Hass in 1923. Addison initially took over for Moore on Moore's retirement, and Vatter and Hass after graduation returned to the ministry.

In the history of religions subsection of the division of history in the Graduate School of Arts and Sciences, George Foot Moore taught History of Religions 20, a course of independent study designed to "direct the researches of competent students." Neither the opportunity given to graduate students to minor in Religionswissenschaft nor the introduction of the Th.D. caused students to become original researchers in the history of religions. Moore had the opportunity to acquaint ministers and graduate students in related disciplines with the findings of Religionswissenschaft research. He did not, however, direct more than a handful of advanced graduate students in significant scholarship who were recognized as contributors to the growing field of the science of religion.

The few graduate students who chose to do a portion of their advanced work in the history of religions were joined by a number of students from the college who were interested in Religionswissenschaft as either one small part of their liberal arts curriculum or solely on the strength of the teaching reputation of George Foot Moore. Charles Eliot's elective system opened up theological classes to all students as part of their liberal arts training and students from the college flooded divinity school courses. In his 1889-90 annual report, divinity school dean Everett mentioned that 183 selections were made chiefly by college students "of courses originally peculiar to the Divinity School, but which may now be counted also for the degree of A.B."[45] Three years later Eliot openly proclaimed, "the School is furnishing a large amount of instruction for College undergraduates."[46]

The divinity school faculty were aware of the importance of nondivinity students for the growth and success of the school's programs. Certainly the growth in the number of theological faculty from 1890 to 1920 was primarily the result of college students filling the ranks of divinity courses. At times the numbers were staggering. The divinity faculty minutes of October 28, 1902 read:

> The Dean gave some statistics in regard to elections of courses this year, showing that students registered in the Divinity School had made 33 elections, or the equivalent of 25 full courses, of courses only offered by the Faculty of Arts and Sciences, and that students registered under the Faculty of Arts and Science had made 248 elections, the equivalent of 247 full courses, of courses offered by the Divinity Faculty.[47]

George Foot Moore's courses in the history of religions benefited greatly from the crossover effect just described. In 1903-04, for example, one year after Moore joined the Harvard faculty, 108 nondivinity students took one of his two courses, Introduction to the Study of Religions or History of Religions in Outline. Although the number of students enrolled in his courses declined somewhat in the second decade of the twentieth century, Moore continued to have an appeal to nondivinity students.

The students who were exposed to Religionswissenschaft at Harvard and Chicago were either ministers returning to class to do extra study, college students taking history of religion courses as an elective, graduate students pursuing higher degrees in other fields, or prospective ministers. Few were good prospects for serious and prolonged scholarship in comparative religion. The popularity and longevity of Religionswissenschaft curricula at Harvard, like Chicago, were primarily the result of the elective system. Students were able to dabble in comparative religion. Their occasional forays into the discipline excited some (e.g., Riale) to the point that they became "middle-men," reading (and occasionally publishing) in the field although they remained ministers. The very few who decided to pursue an academic career in Religionswissenschaft (e.g., Buckley) were rebuffed by an academic system grounded in standard Protestant fields of study.

FOUR

Religionswissenschaft Faculty

The emergence of an academic discipline has as a necessary component the coalescence of a coterie of faculty who share a sense of intellectual and professional identity. Much has been written about the professionalization of various disciplines as a fundamental process in their development. The social and natural sciences have received most of the analysis in this regard, but the humanities have not escaped notice.[1]

The faculty at Chicago and Harvard who taught Religionswissenschaft courses were an amalgam of scholars with varying backgrounds, academic training, and research interests. I earlier noted the nascent discipline's debt to nineteenth-century discoveries in philology, linguistics, and archaeology. The men who gained an interest in the new science of religion at Harvard and Chicago obviously did so from particular intellectual traditions. The degree to which these traditions contributed to or detracted from the emergence of a Religionswissenschaft identity, intellectual and professional, is an important part of the story. Moreover, the extent to which scholars with Religionswissenschaft appointments attempted to push ahead the discipline—at their own institutions or throughout the spectrum of higher education—through research, curricular innovations, and scholarly associations reveals much about its relative strength.

Harvard Divinity School Faculty

A. James Freeman Clarke

James Freeman Clarke, Unitarian minister and nonresident professor (1867-71) and lecturer (1876-77) at Harvard Divinity School, was one of the first men in North America, and certainly the first at Harvard, to take interest in the study of comparative religion. A graduate of Harvard College in 1829 and the divinity school in 1833, Clarke was ordained on July 21 of the latter year. Clarke's many publications conveyed his Unitarian sympathies and the transcendentalism with which he was closely allied.

It was a combination of Clarke's Unitarian upbringing and transcendentalist beliefs that sparked his interest in world religions. He held firmly to the universality of truth and goodness and sought their expression in all persons, cultures, and religions. He admitted in his autobiography that his studies in theology were greatly aided by the realization that "the vital truth perceived by reason is not the same as the doctrinal statement enunciated by the understanding."[2] Thus religions that had different doctrinal statements could, at their core, share the same vital truth.

Clarke's openness in regard to the truth of all religions found its most complete expression in his two-part work, *Ten Great Religions* (Part 1, 1871; Part 2, 1888). Part 1 was subtitled "An Essay in Comparative Theology" and called for the scientific treatment of the facts of religion. Clarke observed:

> It [Comparative Theology] may be called a science, since it consists in the study of the facts of human history, and their relation to each other. It does not dogmatize: it observes. It deals only with phenomena,—single phenomena, or facts; grouped phenomena, or laws.[3]

Although Clarke defined comparative theology quite explicitly, he admitted that the science was in its infancy. He acknowledged the valuable work of Max Müller and Renan, among others in Europe, but admitted that in America "we have scarcely anything worthy of notice."[4]

In the second part to *Ten Great Religions*, subtitled "A Comparison of All Religions," Clarke switched from comparative theology to the science of religion. He again defined the new science with reference to generalizing from the facts of religion but did not claim full-fledged status for the new field.

> Is there such a department of knowledge as "The Science of Religion," or such a method as "The Scientific Study of Religion"? If there is such a method, it must consist in the faithful study of the facts, and a careful generalization from those facts. It must be free from prejudice for or against any system. . . . Thus only can we reach what may deserve to be called a "Science of Religion."
>
> The whole realm of spiritual exercises; the sense of sin and pardon; prayer and its answer; the convictions, trusts, motive-powers, illuminations, inspirations of holy souls, may and ought to be carefully examined, analyzed, and verified. Then

it will be seen what part are illusion, and what part reality. When this is accomplished, but not sooner, there will be a Science of Religion.[5]

Clarke carried both his interest in the study of world religions and a love for natural theology with him to the Harvard Divinity School when he joined the faculty in 1867. Appointed to a four-year term as Professor of Ethnic Religions and the Creeds of Christendom, he lectured on campus two days a week.[6] Much latitude was allowed him in the selection of his subjects although most lectures were delivered under the general rubric of Christian doctrine or ethnic religions. His duties as minister of the Church of the Disciples in Boston and his involvement on behalf of woman suffrage and the antislavery movement limited his time at the divinity school. Thus, according to Sydney Ahlstrom's history of Harvard Divinity School at this time, he had little influence on the direction of the school.[7] It nevertheless may be safely assumed his influence was instrumental in making the study of ethnic religions a requirement for all students seeking the bachelor of divinity degree.[8]

It must be remembered that Clarke's years at Harvard preceded the late-nineteenth-century interest shown in comparative religion by other American scholars and universities. There was nothing in his writing that argued for the place of the science of religion as a distinct academic discipline within universities. Clarke's concern with ethnic religions arose from theological issues and he was content to consider world religions within the context of ministerial preparation.

Clarke's influence and involvement at Harvard came about less from his faculty status in the divinity school than from his appointment to the Board of Overseers. From 1866 to 1886, Clarke was chosen to serve as an overseer each term for which he was eligible.[9] In his role he examined university policy in many areas and specifically recommended broad plans for the future direction of the divinity school.

In 1864 Clarke was made chairman of a committee to investigate the future of the divinity school and was able to present some of his own ideas about a "University of Theology." He wrote to other universities and ministers to gather advice for his proposed recommendations on the enlarging of the work of the theological school of Harvard. What resulted demonstrated his thinking as to the study of religion at a university. Clarke suggested, in his report to the overseers presented in February 1865, that each denomination be invited to send to Harvard its best scholars to present a series of lectures on a particular theological viewpoint. Each major denomination was to be represented so as to give a student the widest exposure to all theological and religious positions. Ethnic religions also were to receive attention through representational lectures.

> If there be such a thing as a university, it ought to have a department of theology; and this department ought to contain professors of every chief school of opinion. What should some of us not give for an opportunity to attend such a school even now? What would not all earnest and truth-loving young men, longing for solid knowledge in religion, not sacrifice for such an opportunity?[10]

Clarke placed the study of religion squarely within the theological school of the university. Moreover, the history and comparison of world religions were part of the larger purpose of broadening the minds and experiences of prospective ministers. Clarke was explicit that Harvard Divinity School students "would rather be preachers and pastors than anything else in the world" and that they "must be encouraged to inquire and think in their own way."[11] The study of ethnic religions enhanced the students' understanding of the unity of all truth in a theological school environment of free inquiry.

James Freeman Clarke initiated the study of world religions at Harvard Divinity School. Although limited in scope and influence, Clarke's lectures in this new field laid the groundwork for a tradition of openness to the science of religion at Harvard. With Clarke's death in 1888, Charles Carroll Everett continued the tradition.

B. Charles Carroll Everett

In 1869, in the tenth year of his pastorate at the Independence Congregational (Unitarian) Church in Bangor, Maine, the Reverend Charles Carroll Everett published a treatise on logic entitled *The Science of Thought*.[12] A product of Everett's interest in philosophical themes first aroused by his study in Berlin in 1851-52 under Professor Gabler, a disciple of Hegel, the book caught the attention of the Harvard Corporation. In the same year the book was published Everett left the pastorate and returned to the institution that had granted him a divinity degree in 1859. He became the Bussey Professor of Theology, and from 1878 to his death in 1900 he was dean of the Harvard Divinity School in addition to holding his professorship in theology.

Everett's interest in philosophy was overshadowed only by what he considered to be the natural culmination of philosophical investigation: theology. Perhaps better said by Harvard colleague Crawford Howell Toy, during his years at Harvard, Everett "devoted himself to the investigation of the philosophic problems which underlie religious belief, or rather to the exposition of religious belief as based on the results of philosophy."[13] As a systematic theologian of the first order, Everett attempted to establish the ground of all religion. He concluded at one point, "Religion, then, is the feeling toward a spiritual presence manifesting itself in Truth, Goodness and Beauty, especially as illustrated in the life and teaching of Jesus and as experienced in every soul that is open to its influence."[14]

Throughout his years at Harvard, Everett expounded his theological viewpoint through a course of lectures in systematic theology. His central theological and philosophical themes appeared in a diverse set of publications that included *The Science of Thought, Fichte's Science of Knowledge* (1884), *Essays on Poetry, Comedy and Duty* (1888), *Ethics for Young People* (1891), and *The Gospel of Paul* (1893). The most comprehensive and definitive guides to his theological position (which also contain the content of his systematic theology lectures at Harvard), however, were contained in two works edited by Harvard colleague Edward Hale. Hale gathered student lecture notes from two of Everett's three lecture courses and composed manuscripts titled *The Psychological Elements of Religious Faith* (1902) and *Theism and the Christian Faith* (1909).[15]

The one series of lectures that was not produced in manuscript form and published was his course on the history of religions.[16] In 1872, just three years after his appointment at Harvard and the first year after James Freeman Clarke's departure, Everett offered a course on East Asiatic religions. Although the title of the course changed in 1881-82 to Studies in the Comparative History of Religions, the basic content and structure of the lectures remained unaltered in the almost twenty years during which they were given. Everett continued the Harvard tradition started by Clarke of providing instruction in ethnic religions. The genesis of his interest in Religionswissenschaft is obscure but it is certain that Toy was correct when he stated that Everett "entered on his duties in the Divinity School just about the time when the new interest in the scientific study of religion began to show itself, and he was attracted to the religions of Asia as illustrations of philosophic conceptions."[17]

No matter what aroused Everett's initial interest in world religions, his prolonged study of the subject related to its significance for the great truths of philosophy and theology. Everett's method, as illustrated in a number of his works, was to describe, compare, and contrast the world's religions in terms of their importance to and relevance for the categories of the reason.[18] He thus treated Confucianism as a manifestation of the religion of the understanding, Mazdaeism and Zoroastrianism as illustrations of religions of goodness, and the religions of Greece as examples of the ideal of beauty. Christianity, finally, was the Absolute Religion inasmuch as it embodied perfectly the three ideas of the reason.

Everett's scheme did not mean he distorted or superficially examined the historical facts of the world's religions. Nor was he unaware of the growing literature in Religionswissenschaft, both in North America and in Europe. His own course in the history of religion was listed under "comparative religion" in the divinity school catalog and as an elective in history in the college and graduate school. Nevertheless, his devotion to the study of comparative religion rested squarely in his desire to contribute to the exposition of the foundation of religion. He was more a theologian interested in Religionswissenschaft than a scholar devoted to the new field as an emerging discipline. Harvard Divinity School dean William Wallace Fenn recalled, "The History of Religions as taught by Dean Everett was an integral part of his work in systematic theology. . . . Thus, from his point of view, the History of Religions was a department of Systematics."[19]

It was perhaps the above bias that led Everett to do very little in terms of academic or administrative promotion of Religionswissenschaft at Harvard Divinity School during his tenure as dean. The increase in faculty and expansion of course offerings took place in areas more germane to theological education, e.g., New Testament, church history, and Christian morals. Everett's most conspicuous attempt at providing a forum for the history of religions was the great number of Religionswissenschaft articles published in *The New World* under his editorial direction.[20] Nevertheless, Everett himself never strayed from theological themes in his published articles and he never chose to review any of the many books on the history of religions that were received by the editors.[21]

President Eliot was saddened when he was informed of Dean Everett's intention to retire. In a September 18, 1900 letter to Everett, Eliot said:

> Of course, the Corporation would prefer to have you give your instruction just so long as you can give it regularly and effectively. Your courses are very

valuable to the Divinity School; and at the best it would be some years before they could really be replaced.[22]

Everett's death in October brought a sudden end to Eliot's request. There was another man on the Harvard faculty, however, who had gained an interest and expertise in the history of religions. Although George Foot Moore would ultimately carry on Everett's offerings in Religionswissenschaft, Crawford Howell Toy's work in the field is an important part of the Harvard history.

C. Crawford Howell Toy

Crawford H. Toy was ordained to the Baptist ministry in 1860 with the intention of going to Japan as a foreign missionary. The Civil War interrupted his plan and he entered the Confederate army in 1861 where he was made a chaplain. After the war he spent two years in Berlin, 1866-68, studying Semitic languages. Soon after his return he was appointed professor of Old Testament interpretation and Oriental languages in 1869 at the Southern Baptist Theological Seminary in Louisville, Kentucky. He taught at Southern Baptist for ten years but finally resigned because of his inability to accept the seminary's required doctrinal position on the infallibility of Scripture. Toy's research in philology and ethnology and his interest in natural science led to his acceptance of the higher criticism of Wellhausen.[23]

Having no academic post, Toy went to New York during the latter half of 1879 to take a position as literary editor of the *Independent*. It was in his small, cramped New York office that Toy received a visit in the summer of 1880 from Harvard president Charles Eliot. Eliot had become aware of Toy through the newspaper accounts of his removal from Southern Baptist Theological Seminary and after a brief visit he offered Toy the Hancock Professorship of Hebrew and other Oriental Languages in the Harvard Divinity School beginning with the fall semester 1880.

Toy's appointment had nothing to do with Harvard's flirtation with the nascent Religionswissenschaft and everything to do with Elliot's and Everett's desire to strengthen the areas of Old Testament and Semitic languages. Toy had a profound love of languages and his earliest research interests, as displayed in contributions to the *Transactions of the American Philological Association* and the *Journal of the Society of Biblical Literature and Exegesis*, were in Semitic grammar.[24] His love of Hebrew in particular was revealed in his publications *A Critical and Exegetical Commentary on the Book of Proverbs* (1899) and *The Book of the Prophet Ezekiel: Critical Edition of the Hebrew Text, with Notes* (1899).

In his annual report of 1879-80, President Charles Eliot announced the appointment of Crawford Howell Toy to the Harvard faculty:

> In May last, Crawford Howell Toy, LL.D., was elected Hancock Professor of Hebrew and other Oriental Languages. . . . Dr. Toy's affiliations were with the Baptist denomination, but he was chosen, without regard to his denominational connection, on the simple ground that he was the most eminent scholar in the Semitic languages to be procured.[25]

When Toy arrived at Harvard Divinity School there was a weak Old Testament department. His charge was to enlarge on the work in Old Testament and Semitic languages. The conditions surrounding his appointment were keenly described by George Foot Moore in an article honoring Toy after his death. Moore set the initial years of Toy's Harvard life in perspective:

> The chair to which Professor Toy was called was by its title and in the intent of the foundation what we should now call a professorship of Semitic languages, among which Hebrew traditionally held the foremost place; and its first incumbent, Stephen Sewall, had in his time considerable reputation for his attainments in this field; but for a good while it had been actually no more than a chair for the Old Testament in the Divinity School. Professor Toy took his commission in a larger way, and laid the foundations of a department of the Semitic languages and literatures.[26]

Toy wasted no time in introducing a number of new courses to the Harvard curriculum. The first year he added Aramaic and in subsequent years he taught courses in Hebrew, Aramaic, Arabic, Ethiopic, Old Testament introduction, Old Testament interpretation, and the Talmud, among others. In what was the most relevant subject for his later interest in the history of religions, he almost yearly taught The History of the Hebrew Religion, with Comparisons of Other Semitic Religions. Some of the courses were listed both in the divinity school catalog and the graduate department catalog under the department of Semitic languages. The addition of David Gordon Lyon, a pupil of Toy's at Southern Baptist, as Hollis Professor of Divinity at Harvard in 1882, made possible a division of labor in Old Testament and an expansion of offerings in Semitic languages.

With the exception of The History of the Hebrew Religion, with Comparisons of Other Semitic Religions, Toy taught no courses in the history, comparison, or science of religion. There is no doubt, however, that by the beginning of the second decade of his tenure at Harvard he had gained an interest in the broader issues of the new science of religion. His research in Semitic languages and religions provided the foundation from which his excitement for the new discipline grew. In the autumn of 1891 he formed the Harvard Club for the Study of the History of Religions, which included a small but prestigious coterie of Harvard scholars and an occasional outsider.[27] This group met monthly to discuss issues of common interest on Religionswissenschaft topics and occasionally to hear a brief paper by one of the members. Interestingly, the group consisted of philologists, archaeologists, anthropologists, and historians; the influence of the divinity school and its faculty was minimal.[28] In 1912, as a belated commemoration of Toy's seventy-fifth birthday, the club was instrumental in publishing *Studies in the History of Religions* in his honor. Nevertheless, the club was more of a social gathering than an organization for promoting research and study on the history of religions.

Toy's enthusiasm and growing expertise in the history and science of religion were most evident in the lead role he took in reviewing new works in Religionswissenschaft for *The New World*. Everett, who taught comparative religion, inexplicably took a secondary role. Toy became interested in the Columbian Exposition's Parliament of Religions and wrote a review of the event for *The New World*. Recognizing that the main purpose of the parliament was the friendly presentation of the religious ideas of the world rather than the furtherance of scientific investigation into such ideas, Toy nevertheless hoped the parliament would result in an increase in interest in Religionswissenschaft.

> Among the more direct results of this parliament may probably be reckoned an increase in the interest in the science of the history of religions. This youngest of the sciences has, as yet, affected only a small circle, partly because its results have not got into general circulation and partly because the people are not prepared for the study of its subject-matter. . . . A certain number of persons will be incited to a sympathetic study of some of these phases of religion. If only a few are led to do this, it will be a great gain. The materials for the study are very great, the number of workers is small. Outside of France and Holland there is little organized investigation of the history of religions. It is however, a branch of learning that deserves all the time and effort that can be bestowed on it.[29]

Toy's familiarity with the key scholars of the emerging discipline was revealed in his *New World* reviews of P. D. Chantepie de la Saussaye's *Manual of the Science of Religion*, Bonet-Maury's *Le Congrès des Religions à Chicago en 1893*, and C. P. Tiele's *Elements of the Science of Religion, Part I*.[30] Most noteworthy, however, was the mention made in the 1893 *New World* of Morris Jastrow's editing of a series entitled *Handbooks on the History of Religions* and Toy's agreement to write the introductory volume. Published twenty years later as *Introduction to the History of Religions* (1913), this volume represented Toy's crowning contribution to the discipline. Its object, as stated by the author in the preface, was

> to describe the principal customs and ideas that underlie all public religions; the details are selected from a large mass of material, which is increasing in bulk year by year. References to the higher religions are introduced for the purpose of illustrating lines of progress.[31]

The book, Toy's last, written after his retirement from Harvard in 1909, was an analytical description of religious phenomena. Although the only book of Toy's concerned with the emerging discipline as a whole, it was preceded by a number of journal articles that illustrated his growing interest in the origins and development of religion.[32]

Despite Toy's later familiarity with and research in the history of religions, he remained first and foremost a Semitic and Old Testament scholar. At Harvard, in addition to founding the Club for the History of Religions, he initiated the Harvard Biblical Club in 1881 for Bible teachers in the vicinity of Boston. A year or two later he founded the Semitic Conference for graduate and undergraduate students. His professional affiliations also illustrated his prevailing scholarly identity and orientation. He was president of the American Oriental Society and the American Philological Association as well as holding membership in the Society of Biblical Literature. His interest in Religionswissenschaft at Harvard was secondary to his Semitic work.

D. George Foot Moore

When Crawford Howell Toy took a one-year leave of absence from Harvard in 1894-95, he was replaced by a young scholar from Andover Theological

Seminary by the name of George Foot Moore. Moore taught two courses that year, one in Old Testament and one in the Hebrew religion. Earl Boynton Wood, a senior in the divinity school and his class's official historian for the year, gave Moore an excellent review in the class of 1895 students' annual report.

> we became better acquainted with Dr. Moore of Andover. Dr. Moore came to us two afternoons each week, lecturing for two hours on the Old Testament literature Wednesday, and for two hours on the religion Friday. His courses were full of inspiration and stimulus. . . .[33]

The students were not the only ones impressed with George Foot Moore. Toy struck up an acquaintance with the Andover professor and when Dean Everett's retirement became imminent, Toy tried to persuade Moore to leave Andover and join the faculty of the Harvard Divinity School. On May 30, 1901, Moore wrote to President Eliot:

> I saw Professor Toy yesterday afternoon and he set forth in an attractive way the possibilities in the field of the history of religions as well as in the Semitic and Biblical work. I am strongly inclined to accept the invitation.[34]

Toy's interest in the history of religions was overshadowed by his Semitic investigations. With the arrival of George Foot Moore, however, the history of religions would be given a rightful and special place at Harvard Divinity School.

George Foot Moore was appointed professor of theology at Harvard Divinity School in 1902. The anomalous title, in consideration of the courses he was hired to teach, was changed in 1904 to the Frothingham Professor of the History of Religions. The Harvard *President's Annual Report for 1904-5* mentioned that the Frothingham Professor Fund had reached the level of $53,203 and the Board of Overseers had decided to name a divinity faculty member to the professorship.[35] George Foot Moore carried this title until his retirement from teaching in 1928. He held the title as professor emeritus until his death on May 16, 1931.

A number of recollections about Moore's arrival at Harvard have confirmed the significance of his appointment for the field of the history of religions. His brother and Harvard divinity colleague, Edward Caldwell Moore, wrote:

Professor Crawford Howell Toy, who had been Hancock professor of Hebrew from 1880, had lectured, from time to time, upon the History of Religions. Lectures upon the subject were published by him in 1913. But, with the establishment of the Frothingham professorship in 1904 and its assignment to Professor Moore, the subject assumed a place of primary importance in the University.[36]

Although tracing the antecedents of Moore's work in Religionswissenschaft to Everett instead of Toy, acting dean Francis Peabody, in his annual report to President Eliot in 1901-2, was equally optimistic about the importance of Moore's election for the science of religion:

> Of these changes the most noteworthy is the expansion of a single course, given for many years by Dr. Everett, into a Department of the History of Religions, announced both in the Divinity School and in the list of courses offered by the Faculty of Arts and Sciences. This new Department is directed by Professor George F. Moore, with whom are associated seven other University teachers, so that there are now exhibited systematically the resources of the University for instruction in Comparative Religion.[37]

Finally, W. W. Fenn gave similar purpose and meaning to Moore's arrival at Harvard when he stated that under Moore the history of religions "became a distinct and independent discipline, much appreciated and widely taken."[38]

At face value, these pronouncements proclaimed the dawning of the new era for Religionswissenschaft at Harvard. With Moore in place, the history of religions, it has been claimed, secured itself as a legitimate and respected field of study. E. C. Moore boldly asserted that the Frothingham chair signified that "Harvard was the first" American university that undertook such an important work as "the scientific study of the religions of mankind."[39] George F. Moore's own experience—administratively, academically, and professionally—however, calls for a much more sobering estimate of the strength of the expanding discipline at Harvard.

Moore's educational experience began with preparatory training at Wyer's Academy in West Chester, Pennsylvania, and in 1872 he received an A.B. degree from Yale University. After a few years of teaching and a year of studying law, he turned to the ministry and graduated from Union Theological Seminary in New York City in 1877. A year later he was ordained into the Presbyterian ministry and from 1878 to 1883 he pastored the Putnam Presbyterian Church in Zanesville, Ohio. He was called as Hitchcock Professor of Hebrew Language and Literature to Andover Theological Seminary in 1883.

During his almost twenty years at Andover, Moore increasingly devoted his scholarly attention to Oriental languages and the Old Testament. His mother had lived for five years in Syria and read Hebrew and spoke Arabic. George Foot Moore likewise acquired a love of languages that he never forsook. W. W. Fenn told the story that Moore once expressed regret that his Harvard appointment, with its concomitant shift in research to the history of religions, had prevented him from writing a Hebrew grammar. When he was reminded that his *History of Religions* would have a much wider readership, Moore shook his head and said, "But I wish I could have written my Hebrew Grammar."[40]

There is no doubt, as Edward C. Moore claimed, that George Foot Moore's studies at Andover "were largely in Oriental languages, then also, in Old Testament exegesis."[41] His publications revealed this orientation. In addition to writing nearly forty articles for *Encyclopedia Biblica*, he wrote *Commentary on the Book of Judges* (1895), *The Book of Judges: A Translation and Notes* (1898), and *The Book of Judges in Hebrew* (1900). His exhaustive treatment of Judges revealed Moore's predilection for precise historical, linguistic, and exegetical analysis of a given subject. He openly disdained historical generalizations and speculative theories.

In addition to the aforementioned publications, Moore's Andover years were filled with editorial and professional responsibilities, again in the fields of Oriental languages and Old Testament. He was editor of the *Journal of Biblical Literature* from 1889 to 1894 and the *Journal of the American Oriental Society* from 1896 to 1899. He wrote a number of articles for the *Andover Review* and was active in the Society of Biblical Literature and Exegesis, the American Oriental Society, and the Massachusetts Historical Society.

W. W. Fenn believed that with Moore's appointment at Harvard "his central interest shifted from the Old Testament to the History of Religions."[42] It would be more accurate, however, to say that Moore's early interest in Semitic languages and the Old Testament was translated into a curiosity with the rise of Judaism and Christianity in their respective cultures. With the exception of volume one of *History of Religions*, which treated the religions of China, Japan, Egypt, India, Persia, Greece, Rome, Babylonia, and Assyria, Moore's central focus during his Harvard years was the culture of Judaism in relation to surrounding cultures. The articles he published in the *Harvard Theological*

Review, for example, centered on this topic.[43] Moreover, his crowning and final work, *Judaism in the First Centuries of the Christian Era* (Vols. 1 and 2, 1927; Vol. 3, 1930), signal- : his "return to a development of his earlier interest."[44]

Moore showed no interest in promoting the science of religion as an independent discipline. He openly disdained authors who used comparative religion or the history of religion to make generic comparisons or metaphysical speculations. He was a historian committed to the investigation of particular characteristics of religious traditions. As his brother stated, "He felt himself to be a professor of history."[45] The *History of Religions* contained his most concise statement of method:

> In religions as in civilizations it is not the generic features but the individual characteristics that give them their highest interest and, we may say, value. It has accordingly been the author's aim, without exaggeration, to bring into relief the individuality of the several religions as it expresses itself in their history.[46]

Moore's review of two works on comparative religion for the *Harvard Theological Review* illustrated his contempt for a comparative methodology without thorough research into particular traditions. In his review of F. B. Jevons's *Comparative Religion*, it took only four sentences to point out the essential flaws of the work. Moore concluded, "But in putting so much into such small compass, qualifications and explanations are impossible, and the concise statements and broad generalizations leave large room for misunderstanding, when they do not invite it."[47] In reviewing Louis Henry Jordan's *Comparative Religion: Its Adjuncts and Allies*, Moore touched briefly on Jordan's thesis that comparative religion must be a separate and independent discipline, discovering laws of religious development from the materials provided by history, archaeology, anthropology, sociology, and related disciplines. Moore responded cynically, "How much more successfully the so-called 'science' of Comparative Religion will deal with them [laws of religious development] remains to be seen."[48]

For Moore, then, the field of the history of religions was better served by scientifically sound research than polemical essays and by careful historical investigation in related disciplines than theological speculation. His courses and his students at Harvard became more advanced and specialized as years went by. He taught many nondivinity students and increasingly directed the research of graduate students in arts and sciences. E. C. Moore remembered his brother's primary influence as being on "advanced students most of whom were preparing to teach" and claimed that by the end of his brother's career his teaching "was addressed more and more to special advanced students who came to him for guidance in their works."[49] These students were not interested in the discipline of Religionswissenschaft per se but rather in history, philology, or Semitic languages. They took the opportunity to work with the Harvard professor many regarded as the most brilliant and Moore greeted all serious researchers with open arms.

It was George Foot Moore's presence and influence that gained a place for the history of religions in the curriculum of the divinity school. Although he also held a position in the faculty of arts and sciences, Moore never sought to promote the study of the history of religions as a humanistic field outside the theological arena. It was his belief that the history of religions was an important aspect of theological training that held a rightful place in the university. This is not to say that he argued for a vocational basis for the inclusion of the history of religion. Rather, as the center of the unhindered study of religion in the university, the seminary should provide for Religionswissenschaft. In an address given before the alumni of Harvard Divinity School in June 1902, Moore spoke freely about the freedom of thought that he believed should be the cornerstone of a divinity school.

> Theology will be as free as other branches of history, philosophy or sociology. The sole obligation resting on every student and teacher will be, as in every science, to ascertain the facts, to apprehend their significance, to think through, and to expound and defend his conclusions without reserve.[50]

Moreover, Moore concluded that the theological school should serve the university by scientifically treating all branches of religion, including the history of religion:

> The University, in turn, is the fit and natural seat of such a school of theology. Here it finds the freedom, the unity of aim and method in diversity of opinion, which should characterize it. . . . The theological school has, on its part, a service to render to the University by dealing with religion—"the most real concern in life"—in such a spirit and method as to command for theology the place which of right belongs to it in the circle of sciences.[51]

W. W. Fenn, E. C. Moore, and Peabody quoted earlier, overestimated the importance of the field of the history of religions at Harvard after the appearance of George Foot Moore. Their exaggerated recollections may have been due, in part, to the almost mythical reverence accorded Moore by his Harvard colleagues. George Foot Moore's personal research agenda was intimately connected to Old Testament and Semitic studies. He was more a *historian* of religion than a historian of *religion*. As such, his academic and professional pursuits were scattered among many disciplines and he felt no compunction to promote the fledgling Religionswissenschaft. Many colleagues and students at Harvard who worked closely with him were in related disciplines. And those scholars who attempted to find a unique niche or special status for the history of religions, e.g., Jordan, were treated harshly.

In the academic year 1917-18 James Thayer Addison was named alumni lecturer on religion and missions at Harvard Divinity School. Only a few years earlier he had received a bachelor of divinity degree from Harvard. In 1917-18 he taught a course on the religions of China and Japan and his interest and involvement at Harvard evolved to the point that by 1925-26 he was teaching Moore's History of Religions in Outline course while holding the position of professor of the history of religion and missions at the Harvard-affiliated Episcopal Theological School. Addison received his master of sacred theology degree from Harvard in 1917 and when George Foot Moore retired in 1928 Addison taught all of Moore's history of religion courses the following year. Despite his apparent successorship to Moore, Addison was passed by when the Frothingham Professorship of the History of Religion went to Albert Nock in 1930. Neither Nock nor Addison approximated the respect or proven scholarship of George Foot Moore.

The four faculty members at Harvard Divinity School between 1880 and 1930 who taught Religionswissenschaft subjects gained an interest in the neophyte field from different intellectual traditions. Clarke's Unitarianism and Everett's theological Weltanschaung played a formative role in their interest in other religions. Toy and Moore, on the other hand, pursued Religionswissenschaft research within the context of an expertise in Semitic languages. Whatever their backgrounds, Everett, Toy, and to a lesser extent Clarke were elected to faculty positions that expressly had little to do with comparative religion or the history of religion. With their primary research interests, students, and academic appointments (excepting Moore) in related disciplines, these men could accommodate those who took an interest in the emerging field of the history of religion without concerning themselves with the need to forge a separate identity and focus for the discipline.

The University of Chicago Faculty

A. George Stephen Goodspeed

George Stephen Goodspeed, born in 1860 the son of a Baptist minister, entered the Baptist Union Theological Seminary in Morgan Park, Illinois, one year after he graduated from Brown University in 1880. At Morgan Park he encountered a young and charismatic professor of Hebrew, William Rainey Harper, who was popularizing the study of Hebrew through correspondence courses. Goodspeed shared Harper's love of Hebrew and desire to make the study of the Bible available to minister and layman alike. Harper found in Goodspeed the serious student he needed to assist him in his increasingly rigorous workload and the two became friends.

After receiving his bachelor of divinity degree in 1883, Goodspeed decided to accept the call of the Baptist Church of Sonora, California. His two-year pastorate in Sonora was followed by a similar stay at the Baptist Church in Springfield, Massachusetts. It was from the latter pastorate that Harper called Goodspeed to join him at Yale where Harper had taken the professorship of Semitic languages in the graduate school. Although Harper thought highly of the scholarly ability of Goodspeed, his invitation was also prompted by the petitions of Goodspeed's associates in Springfield, who candidly expressed to Harper that Goodspeed's talents as a minister of the gospel were sorely lacking. On January 16, 1888, W. H. P. Faunce, pastor of the State Street Baptist Church in Springfield, wrote frankly to Harper:

> I wish that Goodspeed would engage in some sort of teaching or literary work, instead of the pastorate. . . . There he would be at his best, as now he is not. If he ever becomes a successful pastor, it will be through years of painful experience—this last year has been one of them.[52]

Goodspeed entered Yale University in the fall of 1888.

His years at Yale solidified Goodspeed's close working relationship and intimate friendship with Harper.[53] Harper invited Goodspeed to New Haven in part of take over some editorial responsibilities for the journal *The Old Testament Student*. In addition, Goodspeed played a major role in the correspondence courses offered through Harper's American Institute of Sacred Literature and coauthored a number of inductive Bible study lessons with Harper.[54] He officially held an assistantship to Harper at Yale and aided in the teaching of a number of Semitic courses. He received his doctorate in 1891 from the Department of Semitic Languages. His dissertation was titled "The Aramaic Section of the Book of Daniel."

George Goodspeed's love and command of Semitic studies and biblical exegesis were evident from his days at the Baptist Union Theological Seminary. In the initial 1882 issue of *The Hebrew Student* (subsequently *The Old Testament Student* [1883-1889], *The Old and New Testament Student* [1889-1892], and *The Biblical World* [1893-1920]), Goodspeed contributed a half-page article entitled "The Word 'Handful' in Psalm 72:16." With his arrival at Yale he was able to publish, in addition to the inductive Bible studies he coauthored with Harper, "The Twenty-Fourth Psalm: An Expository Sketch" and "The Proverbs of the Bible and Other Proverbs."[55]

Such scholarly interests led Goodspeed to Germany in 1891 and the first half of 1892 for concentrated study at the University of Freiburg. By this time Harper had accepted the call to the presidency of the new University of Chicago and Goodspeed was in frequent communication with Harper both regarding his studies in Europe and an anticipated faculty position at the new university.[56] It was in Germany that Goodspeed became more directly exposed to and excited by comparative religion. On November 8, 1891 he wrote to Harper:

> I think that I made no mistake in coming to Freiburg—all the circumstances being considered. I am making considerable headway in German and am taking lectures in Comparative Religion with a young man but a bright and learned fellow—a Roman Catholic professor. I have also a lot of books on Comparative Rel and Oriental History and am making a beginning in that direction.[57]

Three weeks later Goodspeed similarly wrote, "It is a great joy and relief to turn into the fields of Ancient History and Comparative Religion. Indeed, you may be surprised to learn that I am reading German books in both lines."[58]

In January 1892 the University of Chicago Board of Trustees appointed George S. Goodspeed associate professor of ancient history and comparative religion in the graduate school of the university. On hearing the news of the board's action, Goodspeed wrote to Harper in characteristic modesty, "It is not necessary for me to say how indebted I feel to you for the action in relation to me by the Board of Trustees last month. I know that I am not equal to such a position but I know that I shall do my best."[59] In the ensuing months Goodspeed corresponded with Harper about his course offerings and other administrative matters in preparation for the opening of the university in October 1892. Goodspeed's growing interest in ancient history and comparative religion evidenced itself in his course selections and departmental concerns. He was prepared to undertake a heavy teaching load—twenty hours per week—in order to give adequate treatment to the emerging fields of ancient history and comparative religion. On April 14, 1892, he wrote to Harper that the demanding schedule he proposed was based on the fact that he had "to cover two very large departments; ancient history and the history of religions. Hence to fairly represent both departments, in both of which I am alone, I felt it necessary to offer more than if I had but one department's work in hand."[60]

During the first academic year of the University of Chicago, 1892-93, a student could have taken one or more of ten courses offered by George Stephen Goodspeed.[61] Goodspeed taught six courses in the Department of Semitic Languages and Literatures and four courses in the Department of Comparative Religion. In the latter department he was the only instructor the first year and the head of the department until his death in 1905. In 1892-93 he gave courses in Indian Religions, Religions of China and Non-Civilized Peoples; Religions of Greece, Rome, and North Europe; and Islam. In the former department, much larger by contrast, he was one of seven officers of instruction. His course offerings reflected his interest in the history of Israel and its surrounding neighbors and the first year he taught such courses as Relations of Hebrew and Egyptian History, Relations of Hebrew and Babylonio-Assyrian History, Biblical History: From the Exile to the Christian Era, History of Antiquity, and the History of Babylonia and Assyria.

No significant changes in Goodspeed's course offerings occurred during his tenure at Chicago. He remained the mainstay of the Department of Comparative Religion, his courses being augmented by those of occasional visiting professorial lecturers or docents who periodically joined the department. He continued to play a significant role in the Department of Semitic Languages and Literatures, lecturing on the history of the Hebrew nation, Babylonian-Assyrian history, and related themes. It is of interest that in the Department of Comparative Religion he always left the teaching of the science of religion or comparative religion to an associate and he never published an article or book that served to promote the neophyte discipline. His colleague Edmund Buckley, by contrast, published two essays promulgating the new Religionswissenschaft.[62]

Goodspeed's scholarly orientation was most apparent in his publications. His early devotion to Semitics and biblical exegesis evolved into a love affair with ancient history. During his lifetime he published four books: *Outlines of Lectures on the History of the Hebrews* (1898), *Israel's Messianic Hope* (1900), *A History of the Babylonians and Assyrians* (1902), and *The History of the Ancient World* (1904). He authored over fifteen articles for *The Biblical World* and they all similarly reflected a research agenda preoccupied with the religious history of Israel and surrounding nations.[63]

Perhaps Goodspeed's most direct contribution to comparative religion, in addition to leading and promoting the Department of Comparative Religion at Chicago, was his editing of "Comparative Religion Notes" for *The Biblical World*. Beginning in 1894, the journal occasionally carried information on the health and status of the struggling academic field. This section delineated relevant lectureships, university courses and programs, and recently published scholarly contributions to the discipline. It demonstrated that Goodspeed had an interest in and knowledge of the discipline and the inroads it was making in American universities. The first "Comparative Religion Notes" section of the 1894 *Biblical World* made reference to a proposed Journal of Comparative Religion, which was to be published by Chicago's Department of Comparative Religion to "serve as a medium of communication and information among scholars in this field."[64] The journal never came into existence and for unknown reasons the "Comparative Religion Notes" section of the January-June 1899 *Biblical World* was the last.

It appears that Goodspeed's only essay on the need and value of the study of comparative religion was an editorial in the 1895 issue of *The Biblical World*. Using E. W. Hopkins's argument for the importance of the study of Hindu religions as given in his book *The Religions of India*, Goodspeed outlined three elements of value that are derived from the study of non-Christian religions: the light shed on man and his culture, the inspiration given as the student perceives the transforming power of religion, and the warnings provided through the discovery of shortcomings and religious error. Such a study does not, however, improve upon the theological and philosophical foundations of Christianity. Goodspeed unashamedly stated, "Christianity will give; it has no need to borrow." In this way Goodspeed promulgated the benefit of research in comparative religion within the context of the fullness and finality of the Christian religion. He concluded, "For the Christian thinker Comparative Religion has no terrors; rather it is full of rich fruit. . . . The only regrettable fact is that so few of our ministers and divinity students are awakened to its real importance."[65]

During Goodspeed's years at Chicago he was joined by a coterie of ministers and scholars who received academic appointments in the Department of Comparative Religion. The first was the Reverend John Henry Barrows, who was appointed professorial lecturer in comparative religion in 1893 and held the position until his death in 1902. Barrows was famous for his leadership of the Parliament of Religions at the Columbian Exposition. Although Barrows's daughter wrote concerning her father's appointment, "Probably no other honor ever came to him for which he cared more, and of all the organizations with which he was ever connected few rivalled in his affections the University of Chicago," Barrows's role in the department was extremely limited.[66] As professorial lecturer he typically offered one course a year (usually the Haskell Lectures, which he presented on Sunday afternoons in May and June, for no credit). His appointment at Chicago was secondary to his pastorate at the First Presbyterian Church of Chicago (1881-96) and, obviously, to his presidency of Oberlin College (1898-1902).

The title of professorial lecturer in comparative religion was given to five other men between 1894 and 1904 who similarly gave the Haskell or Barrows lectures on comparative religion.[67] These men were scholars who came to the University of Chicago solely to give a lecture series on some aspect of comparative religion. George Foot Moore, for example, was the Haskell Professorial Lecturer on Comparative Religion during the academic year 1904-05. He presented a series of lectures titled "Fundamental Problems of the History of Religion." These lectures were given on Sundays during January and February 1905, for no credit. George Foot Moore's experience at Chicago was typical of the other lecturers and these men had little effect on the work of the department.

Small student enrollments gave George S. Goodspeed little reason to attempt to increase the number of faculty members in his department. His one request to Harper in this regard was to make Edmund Buckley a docent in 1894, a request that Harper granted. Nevertheless, by 1900 Buckley was teaching only one course in the summer quarter. Goodspeed was the driving force behind the Department of Comparative Religion from 1892 until his death in 1905. He was the one who requested fellowships from Harper, ordered new works in comparative religion for the library, and handled student inquiries concerning program requirements. If there was to be a crusader for the cause of comparative religion, it would have been George S. Goodspeed.

Unfortunately, George Goodspeed's life was cut short at the young age of forty-five. In a memoriam published in *The Biblical World* soon after his death,

Goodspeed's increasing interest in the field of comparative religion was highlighted. Also revealed, however, was his wide-ranging curiosity in all theological subjects. It was this broad-mindedness that provided Goodspeed with a professional and scholarly identity that extended beyond the boundaries of Religionswissenschaft.

> His work in ancient and biblical history is of a high order and likely to possess lasting value. But more and more eagerly in the last years of his life his thoughts turned to the great subject of comparative religion. To studies in this field, in which he had already made large attainments, he longed to give himself entirely; and it is the unappeasable regret of his associates that this life should have been cut short with these hopes unfulfilled. They do Professor Goodspeed an injustice, however, who think of him as a specialist only. So closely and with so sympathetic an understanding had he followed the course of theological speculation during the years since he turned aside from the distinctive work of the preacher that he might easily and quickly have found himself at home in a chair of theology.[68]

Goodspeed's growing desire to give himself completely to comparative religion found an administrative outlet through his plan to reorganize and strengthen the Department of Comparative Religion. In a January 3, 1905 memo to Harper, Goodspeed outlined a restructured department that would be "the center for all the studies of religion in its various forms and fields which the university offers."[69] His plan was to divide the work of the department into three sections and have one full-time professor represent each area. The areas of study were to be the history of religions, the psychology of religion, and the philosophy of religion. Goodspeed was to take the history of religions, George Burman Foster would handle the philosophy of religion after his transfer from his theology chair in the divinity school, and Chicago philosophy professor Edmund S. Ames would treat the psychology of religion.

Only days after Goodspeed wrote this memo Harper received notice from his physicians that he had terminal cancer. The news did not apparently thwart the plans conceived because on January 25, 1905, George Burman Foster wrote in a brief letter to Harper, "I am hereby making a formal request to be transferred to the Department of Comparative Religion to teach the philosophy of religion there. I trust you may see your way to make this transfer."[70] Harper granted Foster's wish, but before further action could be taken George S. Goodspeed contracted pneumonia and died on February 17, 1905. The Department of Comparative Religion was placed in the hands of George Burman Foster.

B. George Burman Foster

Foster's transfer to the Department of Comparative Religion was to be part of a larger reorganization of that department and the Department of Systematic Theology in the divinity school. In his 1904-05 annual report, divinity school dean Eri Hulbert briefly described the reorganization and expressed hope that the death of Goodspeed would not destroy the new scheme despite his central importance to the plan.

> The University and the Divinity School are co-operating in a plan which looks to the reorganization and enlargement of the Department of Comparative Religion in the Graduate School and of the Department of Systematic Theology in the Graduate Divinity School. The plan provides for three chief instructors in Comparative Religion and for four in Systematic Theology. In moving toward its realization, Professor Foster has been transferred from Systematic Theology to Comparative Religion, and has been made Professor of the Philosophy of Religion; and Professor Mathews has been transferred from New Testament Literature to Systematic Theology, and made Professor of Scriptural Theology. The lamented death of professor George S. Goodspeed removes the brilliant scholar under whose headship the Department of Comparative Religion (with which he was identified from the opening of the University) was to have been reorganized, and creates a vacancy it will be extremely difficult to fill. This loss retards, but does not frustrate, the plan originally marked out by the two Boards.[71]

Unfortunately, Goodspeed's death did frustrate the proposal. Although Harper may have shared Goodspeed's desire to strengthen the Department of Comparative Religion, there is little doubt that Foster's transfer was precipitated by his controversial theological views and an eagerness to remove him from the divinity school, where the Baptists could most easily attack him. After Foster's appointment at Chicago in 1895 as associate professor of systematic theology, his liberal views became increasingly known to Baptists through his addresses and publications. By the turn of the century President Harper was receiving numerous complaints about the unorthodoxy of Foster and more than a few calls for his dismissal. In 1904, for example, Rev. Walter Walker, a Baptist minister from Des Moines, Iowa, wrote to Harper, "A great many known friends of the institution feel, and feel very strongly that Prof. Foster is not a safe man to train our young men, along theological lines, for the ministry."[72]

Although the most acrimonious debate regarding Foster occurred following the publication of his *The Finality of the Christian Religion* in 1906, subsequent to his removal to the Department of Comparative Religion, there was sufficient controversy in 1905 to warrant Foster's transfer to the Graduate School of Arts and Science.[73]

Foster's move to comparative religion made it easier for Harper and Dean Hulbert to defend the orthodoxy of the divinity school. The following statement, taken from a March 1906 letter from Dean Hulbert to Rev. C. D. Mayhew of Hudson, Illinois, was typical of the responses of the Chicago administration to Foster's critics:

> A great fuss has been made over Foster. Two or three things ought to be said about it. First, Foster is not in the Divinity School. Second, no Divinity student is obliged to hear one single syllable of his teaching. Third, there is not a Divinity Professor, nor any other Professor to my knowledge, who had declared himself a believer in Foster's views.[74]

Unfortunately, the public relations motives for Foster's transfer and the death of Goodspeed left the Department of Comparative Religion with a systematic theologian unfamiliar and unconcerned with the emerging field of Religionswissenschaft.

George Burman Foster received his higher education in his home state of West Virginia, first studying at Shelton College and then receiving the A.B. and A.M. degrees from West Virginia University in 1883 and 1884 respectively. Although ordained to the Baptist ministry in 1879, he did not obtain the B.D. degree until 1887, when he was graduated from Rochester Theological Seminary. He pastored the First Baptist Church of Saratoga Springs, New York, from 1887 until 1891, after which he traveled to Germany for a year of study at the Universities of Göttingen and Berlin. His study in Europe was undertaken at the request of the officers of McMaster University, Toronto, Canada, in preparation for a position in the philosophy department. He was appointed professor of philosophy at McMaster in 1892 and remained there until he was called to the University of Chicago Divinity School in 1895 as associate professor of systematic theology. In announcing his appointment President Harper described him as "The greatest living thinker in his line!"[75]

There is little doubt that when Foster arrived at Chicago he had already forsaken the traditional tenets of Christian orthodoxy. In a dissertation devoted to the evolution of Foster's theological thought, Allan W. Gragg traced the origin of Foster's departure from orthodoxy to his encounter with Ritschlian theology in Germany during the year 1891-1892.[76] In a later book based on his dissertation, Gragg claimed, "Before 1895, Foster had departed from orthodox Christian theology, and by 1909 he had abandoned belief in all distinctively Christian theology."[77]

Foster was first and foremost a theologian committed to the investigation of the most profound questions of humankind's religious life. His writings during his first years at Chicago revealed his penchant for the deep philosophical problems of religion and his desire to strip Christianity to its essentials. Although all designations are limiting, it is accurate to say Foster was more a theologian and philosopher than a historian. At a memorial service for Foster after his death, Chicago professor of philosophy James Hayden Tufts remarked that Foster studied

> (1) religion as a type of experience, (2) the views of the world and of man which religion implies, and then (3) more definitely the question whether Christianity can be regarded as the ultimate religion—a question which involved in turn the question "What is Christianity?"[78]

Such intellectual pursuits illustrate that despite his long tenure in the Department of Comparative Religion Foster never gained a meaningful interest in the history of religion.

When Foster was transferred from the divinity school his title was changed to professor of the philosophy of religion. He chose to restructure the emphasis of the department similar to Goodspeed's plan by offering work in the history of religion, philosophy of religion, and comparative theology. Foster's course offerings, nevertheless, were strongly oriented to theological and philosophical themes. Although he occasionally taught An Outline History of Religion or Religions of Primitive Peoples, he offered most typically The Philosophy of Religion, Hegel's Philosophy of Religion, Kant's Theory of Religion, and related courses. In the academic year 1911-12, a year in which he gave many history of religion courses, Foster lectured on An Outline History of Religions, Religions of Primitive Peoples, and Religions of Indo-European Peoples. He also, however, conducted eight classes in the field of the philosophy of religion that year.

Foster's orientation to theology and the philosophy of religion is most striking in his writings. He published four books, two of them posthumously. The first edition of his most important work, *The Finality of the Christian*

Religion, appeared in 1906. *The Function of Religion in Man's Struggle for Existence* followed in 1909. In 1921, *Christianity in Its Modern Expression* appeared and the publication of *Friedrich Nietzsche* was unaccountably delayed until 1931.

The theological concerns of his books were reiterated in many articles and book reviews he published for journals, mainly *The Biblical World* and *The American Journal of Theology*. Of the more than forty articles, sermons, and debates that he published not one was even remotely related to an issue or research interest in the field of comparative religion or the history of religions.[79] Moreover, of his approximately eighty book reviews only five were of works published in the history of religions or comparative religion.[80] It is ironic that the head of the Department of Comparative Religion made his strongest statement in support of the study of non-Christian religions in a book review.[81]

Foster's distance from the emerging discipline of Religionswissenschaft also evidenced itself in his failure to attract graduate students into his department. By 1913 the annual register no longer outlined requirements for the Ph.D. in comparative religion but merely suggested that candidates for degrees in the department should arrange their work "in consultation with the instructor." During Foster's eighteen-year stay in the department, he instructed only one fellowship holder in comparative religion, Henry Clossen Gilbert. Gilbert was a fellowship recipient during the 1907-08 year who was registered as a student in the divinity school but did not return the next year. Although Foster attracted large numbers of students to his classes, these men and women were not graduate students interested in comparative religion but rather divinity students drawn to the controversial theologian and inspiring lecturer. Shailer Mathews remarked in his autobiography, "he [Foster] became thus a member of the faculty of Arts and Literature. His students, however, were almost exclusively from the Divinity School."[82]

When George Burman Foster died on December 28, 1918, the University of Chicago lost a great theologian. William Wallace Fenn of Harvard Divinity School stated boldly, "Certainly in this country, no theologian was anywhere near his equal."[83] Unfortunately, the Department of Comparative Religion floundered under the leadership of this great scholar. It is astonishing that not one higher degree in comparative religion was awarded while Foster was head of the department. George Goodspeed's desire that the Department of Comparative Religion become the center of the study of religion at Chicago was never realized. Foster's training, interests, and habits precluded a desire to strengthen the department. James Hayden Tufts, Foster's Chicago colleague, said it well when he summarized Foster's influence at Chicago and his scholarly inclinations:

> He brought to the university a twofold training: on the one hand, his work as a preacher, both during his years of study and later for five years at Saratoga, was well adapted to give him knowledge of religious needs and to deepen his naturally kindly and sympathetic spirit; on the other, his year in Germany and three years as teacher of philosophy at McMaster University disclosed new horizons, and introduced him to methods of critical inquiry. The first training was valuable for his chair in theology, the second was important for this but indispensable for his later field of the philosophy of religion. As the work in this latter department was jointly planned Professor George S. Goodspeed would have treated chiefly the history of religion and Professor Foster the philosophy of religion. The death of Professor Goodspeed threw the burden of both these tasks upon Professor Foster. Instruction in the history of religion although at first undertaken with some reluctance, came to be increasingly fascinating as it brought him into contact with a larger range of concrete religious experience. But his training and paramount interests were in the philosophical and psychological problems of religion and in the bearing of these upon the actual religious life of today and tomorrow.[84]

The sudden death of Foster precipitated a quick decision on the future of the Department of Comparative Religion. Even though the department was under the administrative jurisdiction of the graduate school, Foster's close connection to the divinity school and the fact that his students were principally divinity students led to the following recommendation by the divinity faculty less than one month after Foster's death: "It was voted that the faculty request that action be taken with regard to the Department of Comparative Religion and that the Divinity Faculty be permitted to present a plan for the reorganization of the work in the History of Religion."[85] Such a plan may have been presented, but the immediate decision was to put the department under the authority of an administrative board that included Albion W. Small, professor of sociology and dean of the graduate school of arts and sciences; Edgar J. Goodspeed, professor of biblical and patristic Greek; Shailer Mathews, dean of the divinity school; Andrew C. McLaughlin, professor of history; and James H. Tufts, professor of philosophy.[86]

C. Albert Eustace Haydon

The administrative committee's first decision was to hire Albert Eustace Haydon to continue Foster's course offerings for the winter quarter 1919. On January 15, 1919, Haydon received a letter of appointment from J. Spencer Dickerson, secretary of the Board of Trustees, which said, "It gives me pleasure to inform you that you have been appointed to an Assistantship in the Department of Comparative Religion, for Winter Quarter, 1919, at a salary of $375.00."[87] The committee's satisfaction with Haydon, and perhaps lack of an acceptable reorganizational plan for the department, resulted in the granting of a one-year instructorship to Haydon beginning July 1, 1919, and then a promotion to the assistant professorship of comparative religion with a four-year contract beginning July 1, 1920.[88]

The committee did not have to look far to find A. Eustace Haydon. A University of Chicago student in the divinity school, Haydon entered the university in 1916 and received his Ph.D. in 1918. He wrote his dissertation on "The Conception of God in the Pragmatic Philosophy," and was strongly attracted to the thought of George Burman Foster. Twelve years after he replaced Foster, Haydon wrote in the introduction to Foster's posthumously published *Friedrich Nietzsche*, "George Burman Foster combined intellectual fearlessness with a never-shaken devotion to human values. The successful generations of students who passed through his classroom knew each a different thinker but the same great soul."[89]

Haydon had been a Baptist minister in Canada from 1903 to 1913, after receiving his B.A. (1901), B.Th. (1903), B.D. (1906), and M.A. (1907) from McMaster University. One not to shun controversy, his liberal theological views led to a call for his removal from the pastorate by a number of his parishioners at the First Baptist Church of Saskatoon in 1912. Although he was sustained by a vote of 46 to 30, Haydon finally rejected the doctrinal positions of the Baptists, and from 1918 to 1924 he was a visiting minister at the Unitarian Church of Madison, Wisconsin, while simultaneously holding his position at Chicago.

With his appointment in the Department of Comparative Religion, Haydon gained an immediate interest and gradual expertise in the history of religions. Much more than Foster, he concerned himself with the discipline of Religionswissenschaft and particularly the proper method of the study of religion. Although his books revealed a wide-ranging interest in the general question of the place of religion in man's life, he wrote a number of essays specifically on the science of religion.[90]

A. Eustace Haydon inherited a weak Department of Comparative Religion when he took over for Foster in 1919. It was to his credit that he was able to attract a few students to study with him.[91] His extremely long term of service—from 1919 to 1945—enabled the University of Chicago to continue the tradition of graduate studies in comparative religion begun by Goodspeed and Harper in 1892.

The men who took an interest in Religionswissenschaft at Harvard and Chicago were trained as theologians, philologists, and Semitic and Old Testament scholars. Although all studied and taught at a time full of promise and optimism for the growth of Religionswissenschaft, their excitement about the history of religions arose from factors as diverse as the men themselves. Some hoped the new science of religion would illuminate the foundation of all religion (Clarke, Everett, and to some extent Foster) while others were led to the nascent discipline as a natural outgrowth of their interest in Semitic languages or Old Testament history and exegesis (Goodspeed, Toy, Moore).

Most important, the Religionswissenschaft scholars at Harvard and Chicago did very little in terms of actively promoting the discipline among colleagues at their institutions. Goodspeed's attempt to strengthen Chicago's Department of Comparative Religion was the exception in this regard, but ironically, he did little research and publishing to advance the field. Often an individual offered a few Religionswissenschaft courses while retaining an academic appointment and a professional affiliation in a related discipline. Even George Foot Moore and George Goodspeed, the two scholars who carried specific Religionswissenschaft academic appointments, shared in a professional crisis of identity in terms of the influence of Religionswissenschaft on their careers and research agendas.

We can only speculate on the extent to which the Department of Comparative Religion at Chicago would have grown had Harper and Goodspeed not died prematurely. We are also left to our imagination in surmising how the history of religions under George Foot Moore would have fared if he had transferred the program out of the divinity school into the division of arts and sciences. One thing is certain: the programs of Religionswissenschaft study at Harvard and Chicago were made possible by scholars in related disciplines catching the excitement of the field. Paradoxically, the strength and tradition of these kindred disciplines contributed to an inchoateness of identity that precluded the professionalization of Religionswissenschaft.

FIVE

The Seminary Influence: A Professional Role for Comparative Religion

In 1902, William Rainey Harper accurately predicted the growing importance of the research university for theological study.

> The great theological seminaries of the future will be those which are identified, directly or indirectly, with the universities. The time is already near at hand when the theological seminary, standing alone and apart from other educational work, will not be able to attract even the ordinary students, not to speak of the strongest.[1]

It was in the complex process of the rise of the seminary within the university where a significant part of the story of the weakness and inchoateness of Religionswissenschaft as an academic discipline unfolded. Although Harvard's and Chicago's divinity schools were committed to the highest standards of scholarship, both incessantly struggled with the professional needs of future clergy. The professional concerns of Chicago and Harvard provided a context and justification for comparative religion that ultimately relegated the blossoming discipline to a secondary and ancillary role. At Chicago, it was the importance of comparative religion for missions that afforded a sense of identity and longevity to the field. Harvard's concern for the theological and professional merits of Religionswissenschaft consigned the science to a subordinate position to the accepted theological disciplines. In both cases the professional dictates of the seminary hindered the growth and development of comparative religion as an autonomous, independent discipline.

The University of Chicago Divinity School

William Rainey Harper gradually became aware of the difficulty of maintaining both a practical and a scholarly purpose for the divinity school. The school's role as a center for scholarship was quickly established during the first two decades of the twentieth century and the often voiced concern of the administration was to assure that the vocational needs of the prospective minister were given just treatment. Harper finally came to doubt whether the two purposes could ever be reconciled in the divinity school.

> The interest of the University is distinctly in a School of Theology which shall partake exclusively of a scientific character, while it is also within the scope of the University to develop a School of Theology which shall emphasize the practical side of this work. It is a question whether both of these things can be accomplished in the same school.[2]

Divinity school dean Shailer Mathews balanced this tension throughout his long tenure. In his autobiography, he claimed that the divinity school "had to decide whether it should become a detached school of religion or a leader in a religious movement. As a matter of fact it chose to do both."[3] As early as 1905, in a memo to Harper, he admitted that although the interests of the researcher had been provided for, "Just at present there is larger need of care for the professional side of theological education."[4] Mathews introduced many new programs and people to strengthen the vocational side of the seminary work, including professorships in preaching, missions, and religious education.

As the divinity school's position as an institution for advanced theological research became acknowledged, so too did its role as the center for all studies of religion at the university. Such a sphere of influence did not, however, come about without considerable discussion. George Goodspeed originally presented a plan whereby the Department of Comparative Religion would coordinate all religious studies. In 1916 a plan was discussed that would have created a Graduate School of Religion and Ethics within which a Ph.D. (including a Ph.D. in the history of religion) and a Th.D. were to have been offered.

As late as January 1925, the issue had not died. In a memo to Shailer Mathews, Chicago president Ernest D. Burton asked the dean's opinion as to the establishment of a Department of Religion in the Graduate School of Arts and Literature. Burton's plan would have awarded Ph.D.'s in religion in the graduate school. Mathews's answer was swift and commanding.

With reference to your suggestions as to a Department of Religion in the Graduate Schools and Colleges. As I said rather bluntly perhaps over the telephone, I don't believe it is practicable. Neither does any member of our Faculty with whom I have consulted. We have on the other hand given the matter for a number of months very careful thought and are prepared to make a definite set of recommendations which will in a way meet the very thing you have in mind. . . . I might say that the plan as we have it involves the following general principles. First, the avoidance of building up two sets of religious faculties in the University. To establish a graduate school of Religion would mean just that.[5]

Mathews's argument that the divinity faculty should remain the only group for academic instruction in religion was, in one sense, simply a recognition of the divinity school's significant role in the production of Ph.D.'s. Although Harper's expressed purpose for the divinity school from the beginning was to prepare young men to be ministers of the gospel, from its earliest days the school had as its primary administrative unit the Graduate Divinity School, which offered the D.B., A.M., and Ph.D. degrees. All degrees required a thesis on a theological subject, which was to be "scholarly in character." Master's degrees were awarded for additional coursework and the doctorate required a reading knowledge of French and German, a final examination, a dissertation, and twice as much coursework as the D.B. required.

In the first ten years of the university's history, the divinity school awarded 138 bachelor of divinity degrees, 11 master of arts degrees, and 24 doctorates.[6] The Ph.D.s were primarily concentrated in the fields of Old and New Testament. By 1919, however, the percentage of higher degrees awarded in the divinity school was much greater. The total number of master's degrees conferred between 1893 and 1919 skyrocketed to 362 and the number of doctorates awarded increased to 93. Although 389 bachelor of divinity degrees were awarded during the almost thirty years in question, there was no growth after 29 degrees were given in 1897. Furthermore, the percentage of bachelor's degrees as a total of the degrees awarded by the Graduate Divinity School declined from 93 percent in 1897 to 78 percent in 1907, and to 22 percent in 1917.[7]

As the divinity school's role as the center for research in religion became secure, its graduates were increasingly successful in finding teaching positions in seminaries and colleges. In 1914, Mathews spoke about the placement of divinity school graduates:

> The past year has shown a very gratifying demand for our graduates both in churches and in theological institutions. The number of graduates of the Divinity School who are holding positions in theological institutions as well as Bible chairs in colleges and universities is steadily increasing.[8]

It is significant that even though the administrative and curricular structure of the divinity school did not officially recognize comparative religion as a major field, a number of divinity school doctoral students wrote dissertations on Religionswissenschaft topics.[9] A student with an interest in Confucianism, for example, could write a dissertation about Confucius, receive a Ph.D. in theology in the divinity school, and seek employment in a Bible college. In this way the divinity school's influence touched on the work of the Department of Comparative Religion.

The dominion of the divinity school over all religious studies cannot be overestimated for its significance on the discipline of comparative religion. As the twentieth century wore on, the divinity faculty claimed an ever-expanding role in regard to the academic work in comparative religion and the history of religions. I noted that Foster's courses in the Department of Comparative Religion were largely filled with divinity students. Upon Foster's death in 1918, the influence of the divinity school on the future of Religions-wissenschaft at the University of Chicago became pronounced and explicit.

The divinity faculty made an offer to President Judson to reorganize the work in the history of religions immediately following Foster's unexpected death. Mathews took the lead role in a series of communications with Judson early in 1919. It is revealing that Mathews saw no need to justify the intrusion of the divinity school in the affairs of the graduate school's Department of Comparative Religion. The thinking behind Mathews' proposal was clear: the work of the Department of Comparative Religion was essential for the advanced theological studies of divinity students. In his budget plan for 1919-20, submitted to Judson on January 22, 1919, Mathews wrote:

> The Divinity School at the present time faces a very serious situation in view of the loss of several outstanding men in the University engaged in doing religious work. I have reference particularly to Dr. Henderson and Foster. . . . The death of Dr. Foster leaves us without any instruction in one of the most vital fields of research, namely, the history of religion.[10]

Mathews quickly secured the services of Albert Eustace Haydon to teach Foster's history of religions course for the spring quarter of 1919. Although an administrative committee had been formed to manage the affairs of the Department of Comparative Religion, Mathews's position and influence were preeminent. On March 10, 1919, he suggested to President Judson that an arrangement be approved with the Chicago Theological Seminary whereby the two institutions would each appropriate funds to make possible a new professorship in missions. This would allow the hiring of a man in church history and another in comparative religion to replace Foster. Although the academic program in comparative religion was not formally transferred to the divinity school, Mathews's ideas and concerns significantly influenced the direction of the department.

The growing administrative jurisdiction of the divinity school over comparative religion revealed an underlying appreciation of Religionswissenschaft as an adjunct to a theological education. A full and well-rounded education for prospective ministers and advanced theological students necessitated an acquaintance with comparative religion. This theme was articulated in Mathews's desire for a history of religion museum. In his annual report of 1923-24, he mentioned the need for a museum that would be a laboratory for the study of the history of religion. Four years later he again stressed the necessity for a museum to meet "the needs of scientific study of religion."[11] The data and study of the history of religion came increasingly under the watchful eye of the divinity school even though the Department of Comparative Religion persevered in the Graduate School of Arts and Literature with Haydon as its sole instructor.

In addition to its mission of enlarging the educational experience of theological students, comparative religion came to take on the specific vocational function and purpose of training and educating missionaries. Comparative religion instruction at Chicago had never been devoid of partisans who championed its relevance for missionaries. In 1894, for example, *The Biblical World* described many of the course opportunities in Chicago's Department of Comparative Religion as being of special interest for missionaries.[12] On May 10, 1912, the divinity Faculty Committee for Vocational Curriculum recommended two of Foster's comparative religion courses for students preparing to enter the missionary field.[13]

By 1915, the situation at the divinity school was auspicious for a closer relationship between comparative religion and missions. In December of that year, Shailer Mathews wrote to Ambrose Swazey of Cleveland, Ohio, to ask him to consider a faculty position as professor of missions at the divinity school.

> I have been thinking for some time that I would like to lay before you a matter which I have been considering, namely, the establishing of a professorship on Missions here at the University of Chicago. . . . We have in the University at any one time probably more students for the foreign field than almost any other institution in the United States.[14]

Swazey's refusal of Mathews's offer intensified the latter's determination to provide instruction and guidance to the increasing number of missionaries studying at Chicago.

Between 1910 and 1920 the divinity school was faced with a tremendous influx of missionaries on furlough and students training for the mission field. Mathews welcomed these students and coordinated plans with various denominations to provide furnished apartments for use by furloughed missionaries. He was aware of competition from other seminaries for such students and in his budget request of 1919-20 he reminded President Judson that "this latter field [missions] is one which is being given very great attention in all other seminaries."[15] By 1924 Mathews was able to claim, "The Divinity School is one of the chief centers of study for missionaries of all denominations on furlough."[16]

It was only natural for Mathews to propose a scholarly approach to the subject of missions, albeit within the context of professional training. The missionary and prospective missionary, like the minister and ministerial candidate, were more adequately prepared in a university setting that brought together relevant findings from all disciplines. The results of comparative religion, sociology, psychology, and anthropology, to take a few examples, would greatly benefit the student missionary. The most relevant area of knowledge was comparative religion. Its kinship with missions was explicitly acknowledged in 1921 when the divinity school, in cooperation with the Department of Sociology, organized a society for Research Extension in the Field of Missions and Comparative Religion. Mathews declared that through the society "the Divinity School will keep in close contact with missions and their work and direct them in certain research and obtain information at first hand."[17] The vocational focus of the society was confirmed in a 1924 report on the work of the divinity school, which linked the objective of the research extension to the study of "the complex process of Christianization."[18]

Swazey's refusal of Mathews's offer in 1915 left the dean without a faculty member concentrating solely in missions until the appointment of Archibald Baker as assistant professor of missions in 1920. Baker had been a missionary under the Canadian Baptist Board for eleven years and in the years immediately preceding his appointment was associate pastor of the Hyde Park Baptist Church. His responsibilities were to give historical and vocational courses in missions and to "organize a group of courses given in other departments of the University contributing to preparation for foreign, home, and city missions."[19]

The arrival of Baker caused considerable discussion among the divinity faculty as to the proper relation of the new courses on missions to the administrative structure of the school. It was felt by most of the faculty that the vocational emphasis of the offerings in missions was problematic for the scientific orientation of the departmental regulations and requirements. The solution eventually agreed on was to place the courses in missions under the Department of Practical Theology. In this way, it was decided, they would be given some degree of independence and prominence.

This newly structured role for missions courses gave comparative religion a new administrative niche. In the decade 1920-30, there was a division entitled "Missions" under the Department of Practical Theology. One group of courses offered under that division was "non-Christian religions and cultures." All of Albert Eustace Haydon's courses in comparative religion and a few courses in related departments were listed under this category. Missionary students were directed to the Department of Comparative Religion for supplementary work. Although the department continued formally in the graduate school, there is little doubt that the students who filled the courses were missionaries and their ministerial candidate friends. Even the few students who received Ph.D.'s under Haydon in the Department of Comparative Religion often had missionary ties.[20]

Harvard Divinity School

On June 24, 1902 George Foot Moore addressed the alumni of Harvard Divinity School. His topic was the proper role of the nondenominational seminary. Although his purpose was not to promote his own field of interest, the history of religions, he touched on the appropriateness of Religions-wissenschaft for theological studies. The theologian had much to gain from knowledge of other faiths, according to Moore, but the nondenominational school of theology was not to be a center for the study of all religions.

The field of an undenominational school of theology is not unlimited. It is, to begin with, a school of Christian theology; it teaches the history, philosophy, and ethics of the Christian religion, not those of Hinduism or Mohammedanism, for the same reason that the Law School teaches the law of our own country, not that of France or Russia. The comparative study of other religions has a proper place in the one, as comparative jurisprudence has in the other; the Jewish religion has an importance for the Christian theologian comparable to that which Roman law has for the jurist; *but an undenominational school of theology is not a school of all theologies* or of that abstraction which used to be called "natural theology"; still less does it undertake to give the special preparation required by the religious teachers of other faiths.[21]

Moore's brief description of the proper role of Religionswissenschaft within the seminary was his only published comment on this subject.[22] It is evident that he gave high value to the importance of the history of religions for theologians and ministers. His statement also, however, revealed an underlying orientation to religious studies that lacked a raison d'être for nonprofessional scholars of religion, at least in a theological school. This sentiment was reflected in the history of Harvard Divinity School and was instrumental in assigning a relatively minor, professional role to the history of religions.

The history of Harvard Divinity School is littered with debate about the theoretical versus practical emphasis of the curriculum. The overseers to the divinity school often recommended the hiring of additional teachers to provide adequately for the vocational preparation of the prospective minister. Because of its nondenominational status, the school was inhibited in developing practical courses that were often closely related to denominational liturgy or polity. Although the scientific orientation of the school became well known and appreciated, its service to the church came under increasing attack. In 1916, Harvard president A. Lawrence Lowell reported, "The chief need of the Divinity School and of the associated institutions at present is a more systematic provision for training in pastoral work, and instruction in the social problems with which ministers are called upon to deal."[23]

This call for a stronger vocational emphasis surprisingly did not result in a program of study in missions. In this regard Harvard Divinity School differed markedly from the University of Chicago Divinity School's receptiveness to missionaries. George Huntson Williams claimed it was the absence of an evangelical spirit at Harvard that prohibited the study of missions from becoming "an integral part of the curriculum."[24] Whatever the reason, the enthusiasm for missions curricula was clearly lacking and the only effort made in that direction was the offering of a course by George Foot Moore's brother,

Edward Caldwell Moore.[25] Homiletics, pastoral care, and public speaking encapsulated the divinity school's concern with serving the pragmatic needs of the future clergy.[26]

The absence of significant offerings in missions at Harvard offered little hope for the history of religions to couple itself with the missionary coursework that was expanding so rapidly in other seminaries. Harvard's unique nondenominational and Unitarian-spirited history, moreover, mitigated against such a union. Levering Reynolds, Jr., stated:

> In the American seminary curriculum generally, the comparative study of religion had grown out of the preliminary concern with world missions. At Harvard, however, the interest emerged directly from the Transcendentalist concern to find the common ground of the great religions (as with James Freeman Clarke and Charles Everett).[27]

The history of religions at Harvard justified its continued existence apart from the vocational needs of the missionary.

As early as 1869 the faculty of Harvard Divinity School required candidates for the bachelor of divinity degree to pass an examination in the history of ethnic religions. When George Foot Moore standardized the requirements for the bachelor of sacred theology degree in 1911, a general examination in the history of religions was made mandatory. This longstanding inclusion of Religionswissenschaft was due to its professional relevance, the benefit it held for ministers and theologians. This professional benefit had nothing to do with narrower vocational concerns of illustrating the superiority of Christianity for missionaries or for pulpit use by ministers and everything to do with its liberalizing effect on ministers and theologians who would be intellectually (and perhaps spiritually) broadened by exposure to other faiths. This attitude was clearly expressed by Harvard Divinity School deans, particularly Willard L. Sperry.

Willard Sperry was dean of Harvard Divinity School from 1922 to 1953. In an essay entitled "Preparation for the Ministry in a Non-Denominational School," he outlined those subjects which ought to be recognized in a nondenominational seminary curriculum. After treating the Bible, church history, and the philosophy of religion, he turned his attention to the history of religions. The latter field, he claimed, was not an adjunct in preparation for foreign missions. Furthermore, the study of world religions did not give the student "many ideas of which he can make direct use in sermons or in church work." Rather, the study of Religionswissenschaft bred in the student "proper humility" and "widened his sympathies." It was of tremendous help in understanding the problems of East and West and it confronted the student with the importance of religion in human life and culture. Its primary benefit was a "a sobering and reassuring testimony to the universality of the religious factor in the making of cultures and history."[28]

This liberalizing argument was reflective of the attitude of the divinity faculty. Sperry and the other historians of religion in the divinity school also were quick to point out that their arguments for the inclusion of the history of religions were directed to ministers and theologians. Within the confines of the divinity school, scientific scholarship in religion was the province of theologians, not humanities scholars or social scientists. The history of religions was most applicable to future seminary teachers, not teachers in the arts. The future minister could benefit from the liberating powers of Religions-wissenschaft and it was the business of the divinity school to limit its work to training ministers and theologians. This important distinction and theme were clearly illustrated in the relationship of degree fields and requirements in the seminary to arts and sciences degree regulations.

The 1897-98 divinity school catalog was the first officially to acknowledge that a student registered in the divinity school could pursue the M.A. or Ph.D. under conditions set down by the faculty of arts and sciences. Although the arts and sciences faculty conducted all field examinations and had jurisdiction over degree requirements, the divinity faculty outlined five broad areas of study a student could pursue: Semitic studies, biblical and patristic Greek, church history, theology, and sociology. These were "special fields" within related divisions of the faculty of arts and sciences.

This opportunity for divinity students was, fundamentally, a recognition on the part of the divinity faculty that there was an increasing number of students who were seeking teaching careers. The diversity of academic backgrounds and variety of career goals of the divinity students placed considerable pressure on the divinity faculty to decide many "doubtful cases of registration" in which students sought an academic path more appropriately patterned for arts and sciences.[29] The one thing that remained constant, however, was the divinity faculty's resolve that the training of arts and sciences scholars and teachers was not in their bailiwick. There would be no awarding of the Ph.D. in the divinity school. This attitude was not lost on the student population as was apparent in H. H. Horne's student class report of the 1898-99 academic year. Horne reported that five divinity students had received the degree of A.M. and three the Ph.D. Of the three Ph.D.s:

Though these men will probably be teachers and not preachers, one going to Williams, one to Dartmouth, and the other receiving the appointment to the James Walker Fellowship, it yet indicates in a way the attitude of the School on the problem of the relation of philosophy to religion. . . .[30]

The flexibility of the divinity school in receiving Ph.D. candidates led to a problem. Increasingly there was a substantial proportion of registered divinity students who were not seeking divinity degrees. The first divinity student who received a Ph.D. was John Wesley Rice in 1898, the only divinity student that year to receive a doctorate. Between 1903 and 1910, however, forty-nine divinity students were awarded the Ph.D. Although Everett's, Toy's, and Moore's courses in the history of religions were cross-listed in the graduate school, neither the history of religions nor any other department of the divinity school was officially recognized in the degree structure of the graduate school. Divinity students were, therefore, receiving arts degrees in nondivinity fields of study. When divinity dean William W. Fenn in 1909 responded to Chicago divinity dean Shailer Mathews's request for advice as to the awarding of higher degrees, Fenn candidly admitted the difficulty he was having at Harvard. He claimed the problem arose from the fact that the Graduate School of Arts and Sciences did not recognize theological studies as a division, but allied various departments of the divinity school with the already existing divisions of the graduate school. He concluded, "It has been proposed to constitute a separate group of theological studies which should rank with other divisions as a proper field of work for the Ph.D., but no formal arrangement of this sort has yet been affected."[31]

As a practical matter, therefore, the five "special fields" originally outlined by the divinity faculty for divinity student doctoral candidates were meaningless. The authority and jurisdiction of the arts and sciences faculty meant theological students were receiving higher degrees in philology, Semitic languages, or philosophy, to take three examples. Even after the arrival of George Foot Moore in 1902 and the elevating of Religionswissenschaft to departmental status, there was no opportunity for a Harvard student to specialize in the history of religions and receive a corresponding higher degree.

The fanfare that surrounded Moore's appointment at the divinity school caused some to claim significant progress had been made for comparative religion. Dean Francis Peabody, for example, stated in his annual report of 1901-02:

Of these changes the most noteworthy is the expansion of a single course, given for many years by Dr. Everett, into a Department of the History of Religions, announced both in the Divinity School and in the list of courses offered by the Faculty of Arts and Sciences. This new department is directed by Professor George Foot Moore, with whom are associated seven other University teachers, so that there are now exhibited systematically the resources of the University for instruction in Comparative Religion.[32]

The important word in the quotation is "instruction." It is true that courses in Religionswissenschaft were added to the curriculum and Moore's advancing reputation gave the subject respectability and distinction. Nevertheless, the inability of students to do advanced work in the history of religions and earn a higher degree continued. Religionswissenschaft remained an adjunct, albeit an important one, to a theological education. There would be, at this point, no attempt at specialized training in the new discipline.

The anomaly by which students registered in the divinity school stood for advanced degrees in arts and sciences came under increasing attack from the faculty of the divinity school. By 1911, a provision had been recommended to institute a master of sacred theology degree in the divinity school corresponding to the master of arts degree. Dean Fenn echoed the sentiments of the divinity faculty:

> For many years an arrangement with the Graduate School has permitted students registered in the Divinity School to become candidates for the degree of A.M. and Ph.D. under the conditions prescribed by the Graduate School for these degrees. It is manifest, however, that theological studies constitute an independent group not formally recognized in the regulations of the Graduate School, and therefore it has seemed desirable that there should be a higher degree in theology corresponding to the Master's degree in Arts which should be under the supervision of the Faculty of Divinity.[33]

The institution of the S.T.M. degree in 1912 paved the way for the appearance of the Th.D. two years later. With the establishment of these two higher degrees, the divinity faculty was able to keep many of their brighter students who previously would have sought degrees in the graduate school. Only one year after the initiation of the Th.D., Dean Fenn was able to report the granting of three Th.D.'s, all of whom had received teaching appointments. While it still was possible under extenuating circumstances and with special permission to be registered in the divinity school and be a candidate for the A.M. or Ph.D., Fenn made it clear that "the principle of the

Faculty" was that students registered in the theological school "should also be sufficiently interested in theology to become candidates for theological degrees."[34]

The intent of the Th.D. degree program, and to a lesser extent the S.T.M., was clear: theological scholarship leading to seminary or Bible college teaching in the theological disciplines. This purpose was carried out structurally through the offering of three standard theological fields of concentration for the Th.D.: Old and New Testaments, the history of Christianity, and Christian theology. Religionswissenschaft was not ignored, however. The history and philosophy of religion was officially listed as a subsection under Christian theology. The February 16, 1914, faculty minutes read:

> A candidate's studies must fall in one of the main fields of theological study; namely, the Old and New Testaments, the History of Christianity, and Christian Theology, with the History and Philosophy of Religion.[35]

One might be tempted to see in the history and philosophy of religion subcategory a tremendous opportunity for students to do specialized research in Religionswissenschaft and receive a corresponding degree. It was, unfortunately, a difficult and discouraging path. As an ancillary field of Christian theology, the history of religions was granted neither the academic stature nor the administrative support needed to attract students and nourish the fledgling discipline. I treated earlier the three Harvard divinity students who received the Th.D. in the history of religions and the three who earned the S.T.M. in the same field. It is revealing that for two of the three Th.D.'s awarded, there was contradictory evidence as to the field of concentration.[36] In any case, the small number of higher degrees granted was one indication of the difficulty of the Religionswissenschaft degree pathway at Harvard.

It was surprising that with a scholar of George Foot Moore's reputation, prominence, and influence, the Harvard Divinity School did not seek to make the history of religion a separate and distinct major field for the Th.D. In the eyes of the faculty, however, Religionswissenschaft was not a theological subject and therefore not appropriate in and of itself for the theological agenda of a nondenominational divinity school. As an adjunct to Christian theology, the history of religions suffered dearly. Complicating the problem was the fact that some graduate students continued to do Religionswissenschaft-related research and work with George Foot Moore. The situation got so bad that Harvard was missing an opportunity to train historians of religion. This was most explicitly brought out by Dean Sperry in his annual report of 1928-29, a year after George Foot Moore retired.

> At the present moment matters are so arranged as between this School and the Graduate School that it is difficult, if not impossible, for a man to come to Harvard to do graduate work in the field of the History of Religions with the prospect of a reputable degree at the conclusion of his work.[37]

Sperry's candid acknowledgment of the near impossibility of obtaining a Religionswissenschaft degree at Harvard led him to comment further on the desirability of making Harvard "the accepted center for the study of the History of Religion" in America. The time was ripe to pursue such an opportunity, according to Sperry, but it was not the proper role of the divinity school to undertake the responsibility. To do so would mean to open up the divinity school to students whose interests and goals were nonministerial and nontheological. Although Sperry spoke enviously of the burgeoning enrollments of the theological schools that offered the Ph.D., he proclaimed steadfastly that the divinity faculty had no desire "to fill the School with prospective Arts teachers." To train ministers or teachers of theological disciplines was acceptable, but to educate historians of religion would be a liability to the divinity school.

> Personally I am not concerned to see any factitious increase of the Theological School enrollment, achieved by registering men who are not going to be ministers or theological teachers. Other theological schools are already so perplexed by the increasing number of such men that I am persuaded that we shall be better advised to content ourselves, if need be, with our smaller numbers, but with a single-minded professional group.[38]

Sperry was echoing the sentiment George Foot Moore expressed in his 1902 address before the divinity school alumni. The Harvard Divinity School should not, and would not, become a center for the study of religion. The history of religions was appropriate for the prospective minister but the training of historians of religion was not within the professional purview of the theological school. Harvard's ability to play a significant role in the expanding discipline of Religionswissenschaft was centered in the history faculty in the graduate school, and although certain divinity faculty had much to offer a growing history of religions program, "The School [Divinity] obviously has nothing to say on that matter [history of religions program] and any suggestions as to the academic means of procedure would be, from us, an impertinence."[39] The fledgling discipline of Religionswissenschaft remained in a position subordinate to the professional agenda and purpose of Harvard Divinity School.

SIX

Conclusion

There is no doubt that the nascent university at the turn of the century caught some of the excitement of the blossoming field of Religionswissenschaft. The universities treated herein made special provisions for the discipline, but many others added courses, part-time faculty, and lectureships that touched on the subject. Scholars, perhaps reflecting the contagiousness of the 1893 World's Parliament of Religions, were buoyant about the future of the developing field. Louis Henry Jordan was representative of the spirit of the times when he wrote, "It is clear that Comparative Religion is at last to be accorded that recognition which is undoubtedly its due."[1]

There were, however, more sobering estimates of the depth of the incursion of the history of religions into academia. Morris Jastrow, for example, tempered his earlier optimism when, in 1899, he wrote an article that pleaded for the official recognition of Religionswissenschaft as a legitimate academic field by the nation's universities. Jastrow was distressed that so few colleges and universities had provided for the historical study of religion.

> I venture . . . to enter a plea for the recognition of the historical study of religion as a legitimate subject to be chosen by a student in an American university as part requirement for obtaining the degree of Doctor of Philosophy. . . . I feel convinced that not much progress in advancing the historical study of religion at colleges and universities can be expected from now on unless the question of *official* recognition is seriously taken up.[2]

Jastrow's appeal for official recognition reflected accurately the dearth of meaningful, substantive, and enduring academic support for Religionswissenschaft. Many universities briefly flirted with the developing field. Cornell University, for example, limited its involvement by combining its chair in the history and philosophy of religion with Christian ethics and choosing as the chair's occupant a local Ithaca pastor who had very little interest in the science of religion. Boston University, despite establishing the first chair in comparative religion, at no time gave its students the opportunity to major or receive a degree in the new discipline. It is little wonder that comparative religion so quickly and easily vanished from the curricular landscape of many universities through absorption into related courses or disappeared altogether.

Harvard Divinity School's provision for Religionswissenschaft was meager in comparison to the acclaim it received. Edward Caldwell Moore boldly proclaimed that Harvard Divinity School was "the first" American university to be open to "the scientific study of the religions of mankind."[3] Nevertheless, the Harvard scholars who taught and conducted research in comparative religion usually held academic appointments in different disciplines. Clarke, Everett, and Toy illustrate the point. Furthermore, George Foot Moore's appointment as the Frothingham Professor of the History of Religion proved of little significance in the training of Religionswissenschaft scholars or the establishment of relevant degree opportunities at Harvard. The subordination of "the history and philosophy of religion" by the divinity faculty as a subdiscipline and minor field under Christian theology was symbolic of the immaturity and weakness of the discipline. Dean Sperry's statement in his 1928-29 annual report that it was impossible for a student to attend Harvard and receive a reputable degree in the history of religions was a telling indictment of Harvard's Religionswissenschaft tradition.

Thus the fervor that surrounded the arrival of comparative religion was all too often misplaced and unrealistic. In terms of specific academic appointments, degree programs, and research opportunities, there was little of substance going on to enrich Religionswissenschaft. Even in the universities that took the boldest steps to advance comparative religion, it was not the progress that was striking but rather the barrenness of the educational landscape. Comparative religion's emergence in American higher education was a treacherous and fragile journey.

The difficult pathway that Religionswissenschaft traversed was initially forged, paradoxically, by a new vision of higher and professional education that warmly welcomed the newcomer discipline. Harper and Eliot enthusiastically embraced the study of comparative religion for both minister and scholar. Although generated from different religious assumptions, both men's conceptions of the aims and scientific methods of higher learning contained a sympathetic and harmonious role for the study of Religionswissenschaft. Harvard and Chicago welcomed science and religion and perceived no conflict between the two. A fundamental tenet of the modernist movement thus guided a new university outlook: all truth is God's truth; the scientific method, rightly employed, will do justice to the cause of religion; religion has nothing to fear from science and the university has nothing to fear from religion and theology.

This openness to Religionswissenschaft was not, however, an uncompromising acceptance of the findings of the new science. The welcoming of the science of religion was occasionally accompanied by an authoritative and apologetic predisposition to the superiority of Christianity. Boston University president William F. Warren was representative of this attitude. He believed wholeheartedly in the linking of religion and science but his openness carried with it a corresponding commitment that Christianity would surface victorious from scientific investigation. This assurance was echoed by a significant cross section of scholars and university leaders and provided a sense of security for important university constituent groups. The Reverend George A. Gordon, pastor of Boston's Old South Church, reflected the attitude of many clergy in his 1894 address at Boston University's quarter centennial:

> Boston University reminds the ministers of the city that knowledge is the best friend, not of religion, but of the *Christian* religion; that the worst enemy of Christianity is ignorance. . . . There have been heresies in consequence of universities, but they have been nothing to the heresies that have proceeded from prejudice, from mental stagnation, and from sheer colossal ignorance. (Applause.) We are thankful, we ministers in the city, that we have an institution in the city that reminds us of the central feature of our religion, that reminds us that the torch of knowledge easily blends with the torch of Christian faith.[4]

With the supremacy of Christianity assured, the science of religion was given a hearing in universities which otherwise may not have had the courage to give the discipline a chance. Apologetic and moralistic motives accompanied comparative religion's inauguration at many institutions. New York University furnished the most notable illustration. Chancellor MacCracken's interest in building a "Christian" university melded nicely with Ellinwood's ability to attract ministers to his apologetically oriented comparative religion courses. Warren's courses at Boston University's School of Theology were touted for their utility for Christian, particularly Methodist, ministers and missionaries. The popularity of Religionswissenschaft courses and programs at places like New York University and Boston University was unquestionably related to the Christian utility of the research and coursework in the context of the superiority of the Christian faith.

Although not apologetic in orientation, Cornell University's brush with comparative religion was similarly grounded in a Christian rationale. Its provision for the history and philosophy of religion took place in the context of the cultivation of Christian morality as desired by a major benefactor, Henry Sage. Whether apologetic or moralistic in purpose, the important fact was that many Religionswissenschaft programs arose within a Christian—and mostly Protestant—ethos. At the twenty-fifth anniversary of Cornell's opening, Bishop Doane reflected the sentiment of the times when he stated succinctly, "Christianity is the atmosphere in which we think and speak and teach and learn and live."[5] Although all of the universities in this study were nonsectarian, the prevailing Zeitgeist was Christian in orientation and attitude. It was this Zeitgeist which often welcomed a Religionswissenschaft that gave Christianity a superior status.

Difficulties soon arose, however, with such a justification. As the university became more and more secularized, apologetic and moralistic motives became increasingly unpalatable. New York University professor Abram Issacs's statement that he desired to teach Hebrew as literature, not theology, became the accepted perspective in higher education. Scholars increasingly rejected the shoddy scholarship and preconceived results that often accompanied the polemical agenda of "Christian" Religionswissenschaft programs.[6] George Foot Moore and Morris Jastrow, to take two examples, were especially critical of the narrow-minded scholarship. Jastrow claimed that dabblers in comparative religion were hurting the progress of the field and "I regard the attraction which the subject offers to superficial minds, to those who are fond of taking a little dip into the well of knowledge, as one of its most serious drawbacks."[7] It was ironic that the apologetic and utilitarian orientation that first attracted many students to comparative religion later contributed to the subject's remoteness from the academic mainstream.

Not all Religionswissenschaft programs, however, were grounded in a Christian perspective. Harvard, Chicago, and Penn sought graduate students to do advanced scholarship befitting the new academic standards of the research university. Unfortunately, few students chose to go through the rigors of a graduate degree in comparative religion. Goodspeed, Jastrow, and Moore had difficulty attracting mature students and researchers. The paucity of higher degrees awarded in comparative religion at Chicago, Penn, and Harvard Divinity School is astounding when one considers the reputation of the Religionswissenschaft scholars affiliated with those programs.

There is little doubt that the newness of comparative religion and the excitement surrounding other theological disciplines contributed to Religionswissenschaft's lack of appeal. Shailer Mathews reminds us, for example, of the zeal for Hebrew that engulfed many late-nineteenth-century students.[8] At the University of Chicago between 1893 and 1920, three Ph.D.s were awarded in comparative religion, thirty-six were granted in New Testament and early Christian literature, and forty-four were given in Oriental languages and literatures.[9] The University of Pennsylvania granted twenty-six Ph.D.s in Semitics, thirty-three in Romanics, and fifty-six in Germanics between 1889 and 1927, but only four in the history of religions. Moreover, hope of employment after graduation rested squarely in one of the traditional theological disciplines. Opportunities to teach comparative religion at the undergraduate level were almost nonexistent. Even those who received a higher degree in the history of religions usually secured a teaching position in the fields of Old Testament, New Testament, or theology. University of Chicago graduate Edmund Buckley serves as an excellent illustration of the impediments that confronted the seeker of an academic career in comparative religion.

The few students who sought a Religionswissenschaft degree were overshadowed by the many who took comparative religion courses to supplement their educational programs. These students were ministers, missionaries, and theological and liberal arts students who were attracted to the new science of religion as ancillary to their primary academic or professional interests. At New York University and Boston University, comparative religion courses were populated primarily by ministers and theological students. Chicago and Penn, despite seeking graduate students, attracted theological students and only an occasional arts student. Harvard Divinity School's courses in the history of religions were often populated by college students choosing the session as an elective; the remainder were divinity students seeking a S.T.B. or possibly a Th.D. Harvard divinity student Franklin Riale's characterization of his Religionswissenschaft interest as that of a "middle-man, not an original investigator" is a prototypical description of the turn-of-the-century Religionswissenschaft student. No matter whether the academic program in comparative religion was established with academic or professional motives, students considered it an adjunct to their educational priorities and career.

The adjunct, ancillary status of the study of the history of religions applied equally to faculty who researched and lectured in the new field. Jastrow alone recognized and repeated the need for official recognition of Religions-

127

wissenschaft by the nation's universities. His personal attempts to promote research and a sense of identity for the discipline were remarkable. Most noteworthy was his futile endeavor to organize a scholarly association for the history of religion as a division of the American Oriental Society.[10] But Jastrow's voice was the lone cry in the wilderness. Other scholars who took interest in the fledgling discipline were anchored academically and professionally in related but separate areas of study. Most of the scholarship of men teaching Religionswissenschaft courses was in a different discipline. The fact that Crawford Howell Toy's History of Religions Club at Harvard was an informal, social gathering of scholars casually interested in Religionswissenschaft lends insight into the status of the field. The vibrant but struggling science of religion lacked a coterie of faculty members with a common professional identity. The professionalization of Religionswissenschaft scholars never materialized.

Faculty, students, and university leadership all shared a common orientation to the science of religion: Religionswissenschaft was an acceptable, and often desirable, component of a theological education. Although many believed the study was also appropriate as a liberal arts elective, Religionswissenschaft was fundamentally valued and offered for its professional benefits. In the case of New York University and Boston University, the esteem was directed to the utility of the discipline for conservative Christian ministers and missionaries. At Harvard and Chicago, it was included for its role as part of a well-rounded theological education.

The degree of the professional and vocational desirability of the science of religion can be seen in its inextricable linking with the rise of the seminary within the university. As the theological school within the emerging university became the place to study religion, Religionswissenschaft became subject to the particular curricular structure, objectives, and ethos of the seminary. At Boston and Harvard, comparative religion was always offered as part of the theological school's curriculum. Such an arrangement made it easy for Boston eventually to subsume comparative religion under missions and Harvard Divinity School to shun the awarding of a higher degree in the history of religion that would train teachers and scholars.

Even institutions, however, that housed comparative religion in arts and sciences could not escape the widening purview of the seminary. Missionaries and other divinity students made possible the longevity of Chicago's Department of Comparative Religion in the graduate school through course selections and an occasional Ph.D. seeker. At the University of Pennsylvania,

Jastrow's courses in the history of religions came to be taught by visiting professors from surrounding Philadelphia divinity schools. This made the program more attractive to local pastors who were the ones who increasingly became degree seekers after Jastrow's death. The divinity influence was easily recognized in the 1932 change of Jastrow's History of Religions course to a course entitled Outline of Non-Christian Religions.

When George Foot Moore retired in 1928, Harvard divinity dean Willard Sperry was confronted with finding a suitable replacement to fill the Frothingham Professorship of the History of Religion. In his annual report of 1928-29, Sperry raised the question of the purpose of the Frothingham chair. If the aim was primarily to provide training to prospective ministers as a member of the theological faculty, one type of individual should be sought. If, on the other hand, the Frothingham professorship was to be dedicated to the organization of the field of the history of religions, a different type of scholar was demanded. Sperry concluded that he desired that the Frothingham professorship be committed to instruction for prospective ministers or theological professors. Although Harvard had the resources to organize a first-rate center for scholarship in Religionswissenschaft, the divinity school's role, and the Frothingham professorship's role, was to be secondary. According to Sperry, the divinity school should be content to commit itself, as it historically had done, to a "single-minded professional group."

Sperry's position revealed the tendency that this book has illustrated, the inability of Religionswissenschaft to separate from the theological and professional concerns of the nascent university, particularly the rising seminary within the university. A theological agenda accompanied the entrance of comparative religion in American higher education despite arguments, some rhetorical and some sincere, that the new discipline was objective, scientific, and appropriate as a liberal arts subject. Students valued the new science of religion for its professional utility; few even considered its potential as a discipline coterminous with other humanities disciplines.

Comparative religion's emergence in American universities was inchoate and accompanied by occasional apologetic and moralistic motives. Its success, in terms of student enrollment, was due to the interest it held for ministers and theological students. It failed to garner a group of professional academicians with a Religionswissenschaft identity. It was, in short, hindered in its development by its auxiliary role for the professional training of theologians and ministers. An academic, humanistically based identity eluded its grasp until after World War II.

Notes

INTRODUCTION

1. Laurence R. Veysey, *The Emergence of the American University* (Chicago: University of Chicago Press, 1965), p. 2. The literature on the revolution that took place in American higher education in the late nineteenth century is extensive. Veysey's work is an important treatment. Three other significant books are: Richard Hofstadter and Walter Metzger, *The Development of Academic Freedom in the United States* (New York: Columbia University Press, 1955); Christopher Jencks and David Riesman, *The Academic Revolution* (Garden City, N.Y.: Doubleday, 1968); and Frederick Rudolph, *The American College and University: A History* (New York: Random House, 1961).
2. Between 1870 and 1900 graduate enrollments increased from 50 to almost 6,000 students.
3. The rise of the professional schools is an important part of the story of the emergence of the American university. No longer would birth or wealth alone determine entrance into the professions of society. Law, medicine, and to a lesser extent divinity truly became "learned" professions and the professional schools played an important role in enhancing the preprofessional orientation of the undergraduate curriculum. The role of the university-affiliated divinity schools as legitimizers of knowledge is an important aspect of the challenge of modernism to religious orthodoxy. The most visible response of the traditionalists was the establishment of new fundamentalist seminaries.
4. Cynthia E. Russett claims, "It was the misfortune of organized religion at this particular juncture in its history [post-Civil War America] to be undergoing a triple intellectual assault—from Biblical criticism, from the comparative study of religions, and from Darwinian biology" (*Darwin in America: The Intellectual Response, 1865-1912* [San Francisco: W. H. Freeman & Co., 1976], p. 25).
5. For a description of the basic tenets of liberal theology see Sydney E. Ahlstrom, *A Religious History of the American People* (New Haven: Yale University Press, 1972), pp. 779-83. See also William R. Hutchinson, *The Modernist Impulse in American Protestantism* (Cambridge: Harvard University Press, 1976).
6. The *Bethlehem* (Pennsylvania) *Globe* newspaper, on November 20, 1902, reported Morris Jastrow's view on the unity of religions: "Prof. Morris Jastrow, Jr., of the University of Pennsylvania, contributed interestingly to the discussion at the conference of religion in New York yesterday on the question of religious

unity. Prof. Jastrow said that the differences in religion were largely due to environment. . . . The new method [of realizing religious unity] should be by the study of religions, one by another, and by the keeping of our minds open for new interpretations of truth, and for the recognition of varying religious forms as different attempts to express truth."

7. Eric Sharpe, *Comparative Religion: A History* (New York: Scribner, 1975), p. xi.

8. For a good discussion on the significance of archaeological discoveries for the history of religions, see Jan de Vries, *Perspectives in the History of Religions*, trans. Kees W. Bolle (Berkeley: University of California Press, 1967), pp. 66-79.

9. The best treatment of the changes that transformed eighteenth- and nineteenth-century philology and how those changes were appropriated by American scholars is Carl Diehl, *Americans and German Scholarship, 1770-1870* (New Haven: Yale University Press, 1978).

10. Sharpe, *Comparative Religion*, p. 31.

11. The first university chair of the history of religions was founded in Geneva in 1873 and in 1876 four similar chairs were established in Holland. France followed in 1879 with a chair at the Collège de France and in 1884 Brussels instituted a chair of the history of religions at the Free University of Brussels.

12. I have been unable to locate a comprehensive bibliography of the publications of Tiele or Reville. Of their works that have been translated into English, the most relevant are: Cornelius P. Tiele, *Elements of the Science of Religion*, 2 vols. (New York: C. Scribner's Sons, 1896-99); Albert Reville, *Prolegomena of the History of Religions*, trans. A. S. Squire (London: Williams & Norgate, 1884).

13. Louis H. Jordan, *Comparative Religion: A Survey of Its Recent Literature* (London: Oxford University Press, 1910), p. 129.

14. Two excellent collections of essays on this subject are: Alexandra Oleson and John Voss, eds., *The Organization of Knowledge in Modern America, 1860-1920* (Baltimore: Johns Hopkins University Press, 1979), and Merle Curti, ed., *American Scholarship in the Twentieth Century* (Cambridge: Harvard University Press, 1953).

15. For a good account of the post-World War II growth in the study of religion in higher education, see Claude Welch, *Graduate Education in Religion* (Missoula: University of Montana Press, 1971) and idem, *Religion in the Undergraduate Curriculum: An Analysis and Interpretation* (Washington, D.C.: Association of American Colleges, 1971).

16. See Willard Oxtoby, "Religionswissenschaft Revisited," in *Religions in Antiquity, Essays in Memory of E. R. Goodenough*, ed. Jacob Neusner (Leiden: E. J. Brill, 1968), pp. 590-608.

17. Joseph M. Kitagawa, "The History of Religions in America," in *The History of Religions: Essays in Methodology*, eds. Mircea Eliade and Joseph Kitagawa (Chicago: University of Chicago Press, 1959), pp. 1-30.

18. Kitagawa suggests that four criticisms were made of Religionswissenschaft. All reflect the movement toward theological approaches and methodologies. (1) Historians of religion are—should be—really philosophers of religion. (2) The

objective approach of Religionswissenschaft is not objective enough. (3) Historians of religion do not (but should) take into account subjective elements. (4) The historian of religion is conditioned by his background, making the scientific approach less feasible.

19. Joseph M. Kitagawa, "The 1893 World's Parliament of Religions and Its Legacy," pamphlet printed by the University of Chicago Divinity School and Baptist Theological Union, n.d., p. 11.

20. Erwin R. Goodenough, "Religionswissenschaft," *Numen* 6 (1959): 77-95.

21. Sharpe, *Comparative Religion*, p. 138.

22. Kitagawa, Sharpe, and Goodenough all have as one of their primary tasks an investigation into the past methodologies employed by and the current methodologies most appropriate to Religionswissenschaft. The issue of *how* to study religion, and the possibility of a genuine science of religion, are issues that are as important today as they were in the late nineteenth century.

23. In one of a collection of essays devoted to the emerging academic disciplines at the turn of the century, Charles Rosenberg claims that American historians are exhibiting a growing interest in the social context of knowledge and are arriving at the consensus that "even the internal logic of formal thought can be shaped by social needs and assumptions; the domain of seemingly value-free inquiry grows even smaller" (Charles Rosenberg, "Toward an Ecology of Knowledge: On Discipline, Context and History," in *Organization of Knowledge*, ed. Oleson and Voss, p. 441).

CHAPTER ONE

1. Brown University's claim was exaggerated. Its chair was entitled Natural Theology. Neither Brown nor its faculty was given much mention in other surveys of the academic progress of Religionswissenschaft.

   Harvard's absence is accounted for by the fact that George Foot Moore's appointment as professor of the history of religions followed soon after Jordan's survey. Jordan nevertheless recognized Harvard's contribution by admitting that "in fact, if not in name, Harvard already possesses Chairs of the kind called for by these statistics" (Louis H. Jordan, *Comparative Religion: Its Genesis and Growth* [Edinburgh: T. & T. Clark, 1905], p. 593).

2. *Historical Register of Boston University, Fifth Decennial Issue, 1869-1911* (Boston: University Press, 1911), p. 14.

3. Warren O. Ault, *Boston University: The College of Liberal Arts, 1873-1973* (Boston: Boston University Press, 1973), p. 8.

4. *Christian Advocate and Journal*, June 1857.

5. On the occasion of the conference's 1899 visit to Boston's School of Theology, the ministerial committee found the school "loyal to the spirit and doctrines of Methodism." They further wrote, "We also call the attention of young men seeking to prepare for the ministry to the Boston University School of Theology.

You can find no better school in which to fit yourselves for the gospel ministry" (Boston University, *President's Annual Report, 1898-99* [Boston: University Press, 1900], p. 38). It should also be noted that the Board of Education of the Methodist Episcopal Church annually gave scholarships and loans to Boston's theological students.

6. Ibid., *1880-81* (Boston), pp. 26-27.

7. Ibid., *1895-96* (Boston), p. 12.

8. William F. Warren, *The Religions of the World and the World-Religion* (New York: Eaton & Mains, 1911), p. xiii.

9. Warren's familiarity with many of the Semitics scholars, Orientalists, and theologians of his day went beyond mere book knowledge. He actively participated in the American Oriental Society and the 1893 Parliament of Religions. The collection of his personal papers at the Boston University archives contain correspondence with such men as Harvard's Crawford H. Toy and David G. Lyon, C. P. Tiele, and Yale's Edward W. Hopkins.

10. Warren, *Religions of the World*, p. 20.

11. "Boston University: School of Theology," *Zion's Herald*, June 7, 1893.

12. *President's Annual Report, 1895-96* (Boston), p. 35.

13. For a list of the regulations governing the granting of the doctor of sacred theology degree see ibid., *1889-90* (Boston), pp. 53-56.

14. *Inauguration of Lemuel Herbert Murlin, D.D., L.L.D., as President of Boston University, October 20, 1911* (Boston: University Press, 1911), pp. 34-35.

15. Richard Morgan Cameron, "Boston University, School of Theology: 1839-1968," *Nexus* 11 (May 1968): 45.

16. Andrew Dickson White, *My Reminiscences of Ezra Cornell* (Ithaca: University Press, 1890), p. 42.

17. In his history of Cornell University, Morris Bishop relates that White was many times considered for the candidacy for the governorship of New York and once for the Republican presidential nomination at the Republican Convention of 1884. White's major drawback, according to Morris, was his unsoundness in regard to religion. Although he called himself a Christian, White was never confirmed and he refused to accept any doctrinal statement. Herein he was allied closely with Ezra Cornell. See Morris Bishop, *A History of Cornell* (Ithaca: Cornell University Press, 1962), pp. 46-47.

18. Andrew Dickson White, "Address at the Inauguration of the First President of Cornell University," in *Account of the Proceedings at the Inauguration* (Ithaca: University Press, 1869), p. 8.

19. Ezra Cornell, "Address at the Inauguration of the First President of Cornell University," in *Account of the Proceedings at the Inauguration*, p. 4.

20. For an excellent discussion of the politics involved in the passing of the bill in the New York Assembly and the relative roles of Cornell and White in the process, see Bishop, *History of Cornell*, pp. 50-68.

21. D. Willard Fiske, professor of north European languages, librarian, and the director of the university press, mentioned Sage Chapel, the Sage University Preachers, the University Christian Association, and the influence of the

clergymen of Ithaca in making the point that Cornell University was not "anti-Christian" in its tendencies. See D. Willard Fiske, *Memorials of Willard Fiske, III, The Lecturer* (Boston: Richard G. Badger, 1922), pp. 80-81.

22. Quoted in Thomas Hewett, *Cornell University: A History*, 2 vols. (New York: University Publishing Society, 1905), 2:67.
23. Ibid., p. 70. Hewett admits that work in Christian ethics was "the nucleus of Mr. Sage's original plan for the [philosophy] department" (p. 71).
24. Jean Reville, "The Role of the History of Religions in Modern Religious Education," *The New World* 1 (1892): 510.
25. Jordan, *Comparative Religion: Genesis*, p. 383.
26. Morris Jastrow, Jr., "The Historical Study of Religions in Universities and Colleges," *The New World* 20 (1899): 317.
27. Hewitt, *Cornell*, 2:93.
28. For a listing of Cornell's Sage School of Philosophy Ph.D. graduates between 1891 and 1904 and their subsequent teaching positions, see ibid., pp. 77-80.
29. A listing of the 1831 act that incorporated New York University can be found in Joshua L. Chamberlain, ed., *Universities and Their Sons: New York University* (Boston: R. Herdon Co., 1901), p. 61.
30. For a historical account of this issue, see Theodore F. Jones, ed., *New York University: 1832-1932* (New York: University Press, 1933), pp. 16-17.
31. Ibid., p. 65.
32. Chamberlain, *Universities and Their Sons*, p. 142.
33. Jones, *New York University*, p. 65.
34. Quoted in ibid., p. 138.
35. "1893 Report of the Presbyterian Synod's Committee of Visitation to the University of the City of New York," New York University archives.
36. Quoted in Jones, *New York University*, p. 138.
37. MacCracken's position on the governance and spirit of New York University was often marked by equivocation. On occasion he remarked that New York University never thought it desirable to invite Catholics or Jews to form a portion of its governing board and that it was desirable that the university continue to be allied with Puritan elements of society. Such remarks led to a letter of harsh criticism from Dr. Morris Loeb, a prominent Jewish citizen and faculty member at New York University. MacCracken responded to Loeb in an October 5, 1904, letter that said, "I cannot agree that my remarks indicate that I hold that the Council of New York University ought never to elect a Jew or Catholic as a member. I have held nothing of the sort. I at one time urged a prominent Jewish citizen for election as a member but the committee all preferred another name. I have stood squarely on the platform that religious opinion must not debar any person from being elected to a position in New York University." MacCracken to Loeb, October 5, 1904, New York University archives.
38. *Annual Report for 1897* (New York), p. 59.
39. *The University Quarterly* (New York: University Press, 1887), p. 24.
40. Ibid., p. 25.

41. *Quadrennial Report of the Chancellor, 1901* (New York: University Press, 1901), p. 57.
42. Frank F. Ellinwood, "Comparative Religion," typewritten annual report of 1894-95, n.d., New York University archives.
43. *Special Announcement to the 1887-1888 University Catalogue of the University of the City of New York* (New York: University Press, 1888), p. 1.
44. Isaacs to MacCracken, September 4, 1905, New York University archives. (Italics mine.)
45. "Proposed Basis or Terms of Voluntary Agreement Between the University of the City of New York, and The Union Theological Seminary of the City of New York," n.d., New York University archives.
46. The Reverend Robert Booth abstained because he wanted more time to think about article two of the agreement, which provided that New York University confer on alumni of the seminary the degree of doctor of divinity.
47. Hastings to MacCracken, July 10, 1896, New York University archives.
48. Mary G. Ellinwood, Frank F. Ellinwood's daughter, in her biography of her father, candidly referred to his failing health during the years he was associated with New York University. Weakness finally overtook him: "In spite of failing powers, Dr. Ellinwood had been loath to give up his lectures on Comparative Religions; but in the spring of 1903, he was compelled to resign; and was appointed Professor Emeritus." See Mary G. Ellinwood, *Frank Field Ellinwood* (New York: Fleming H. Revell Co., 1911), p.125.

    A press release from the university in October 1902 confirmed Ellinwood's sickliness: "The apprehensions that existed a few months since the Professor Ellinwood might be obliged to give up his graduate work in Comparative Religion have been happily dispelled. His vacation has brought back his vigor, and he will lecture as heretofore." New York University archives.
49. Examples are: James Palmer, pastor of the Manor Church in New York City, "The Practical Content of the Ontological Proof of the Existence of God" (1903); Lewis Leary, pastor of the Huguenot Memorial Church in Pelham Manor, New York, "The Cosmology of the Old Testament" (1905); Charles Hesselgrave, pastor of the Congregational Church in Chatham, New York, "The Hebrew Personification of Wisdom" (1909); and Thomas Gallagher, pastor of the First Methodist Episcopal Church in Eldora, Iowa, "The History of the Sunday School Curriculum" (1914).
50. M. G. Ellinwood, *Ellinwood*, pp. 218-19.
51. The University of Pennsylvania traces its origin to the Charity School organized by the citizens of Philadelphia in 1740. The orderly transfer of power and property to the academy in 1749 was followed by the granting of the first charter in 1753 and a second charter in 1755 by which the academy was made The College of Philadelphia and given the power to confer degrees. In 1779 the charter rights and privileges were absorbed by a new entity called The Trustees of the University of the State of Pennsylvania and in 1791 the trustees of the Charity School and academy and the college and university were granted a new charter, which incorporated the institution as The University of Pennsylvania.

52. Edward Potts Cheyney, *History of the University of Pennsylvania: 1740-1940* (Philadelphia: University of Pennsylvania Press, 1940), p. 33.

53. Cyrus H. Gordon, *The Pennsylvania Tradition of Semitics* (Atlanta: Scholars Press, 1986), p. 4.

54. Ibid.

55. The three courses were Interpretation of the Prophetic Book of the Old Testament, Interpretation of the Historical Books of the Old Testament, and Introduction to the Old Testament. See *Catalogue of the University of Pennsylvania, 1902-03* (Philadelphia: University Press, 1902), p. 217.

56. The two articles were: Morris Jastrow, "Cornelius Petrus Tiele: In Commemoration of His Seventieth Birthday," *The Open Court* 14 (1900): 728-33 and idem, "Cornelius Petrus Tiele," *The Independent* 54 (1902): 510-12.

57. Gordon, *Pennsylvania Tradition*, p. 7.

58. For an interesting account of Jastrow's possible motivations in rejecting the ministry, see Harold S. Wechsler, "Pulpit or Professorate: The Case of Morris Jastrow," *American Jewish History* 74 (June 1985): 338-55.

59. Morris Jastrow, Jr., "The Present Status of Semitic Studies in This Country," *Hebraica* 2 (1888-89): 77.

60. The graduate program in Semitics at Penn was organized as a specific field of study in 1897-98 when Semitic languages was offered as one of sixteen "Groups" of graduate studies. That year a student could have majored in Assyrian, Arabic, Ethiopic, Hebrew, or Syriac under the Semitic languages group. In 1909-10 the group name was officially changed to Semitic languages and archaeology, and Aramaic was added as a sixth major.

61. Between 1892 and 1921 the University of Pennsylvania awarded twenty-five Ph.D.'s in Semitics. For a listing, see *Doctors of Philosophy of the Graduate School: 1889-1927* (Philadelphia: University Press, 1927), pp. 110-13.

62. Morris Jastrow, Jr., "Recent Movements in the Historical Study of Religions in America," *The Biblical World* 1 (1893): 24-32.

63. Ibid., p. 31.

64. Morris Jastrow, Jr., "The Scope and Method of the Historical Study of Religions," in *Memoirs of the International Congress of Anthropology*, ed. C. Staniland Wake (Chicago: Schulte Publishing Co., 1894), pp. 294-95.

65. Jastrow also attended the First International Congress for the History of Religions held in Paris in 1900. He previewed the First Congress in *The International Journal of Ethics*, July 1900, pp. 503-9 and reviewed the Third Congress in *The Nation*, October 1, 1908, pp. 308-11.

66. *Dictionary of American Biography*, 1933 ed., s.v. "Morris Jastrow."

67. See Jastrow, "Recent Movement," p. 26.

68. *Catalogue, 1894-95* (Pennsylvania), p. 167.

69. Morris Jastrow, Jr., "The Historical Study of Religions at the University of Pennsylvania," *Old Penn*, March 11, 1911, p. 645.

70. Ibid., p. 647.

71. For a listing of all doctorates awarded by the University of Pennsylvania between 1889 and 1927, see *Doctors of Philosophy of the Graduate School: 1889-1927*.

72. In 1918, the faculty of the group of the history of religions published a series of lectures that they had given during the winter of the 1916-17 academic year. The lectures had aroused such interest and enthusiasm that they were published under the title *Religions of the Past and Present*. Edited by James A. Montgomery, chairman of the group that year, different religions were treated by the faculty who had made a specialty of that field. Jastrow contributed the chapters "The Religion of Babylonia and Assyria" and "Mohammedanism." See James A. Montgomery, ed., *Religions of the Past and Present* (Philadelphia: J. B. Lippincott Co., 1918).

73. *University of Pennsylvania, Report of the Acting Provost for the Years 1920-21 and 1921-22* (Philadelphia: University Press, 1922), p. 25.

74. In Cyrus Gordon's tribute to the work and influence of his teacher George A. Barton, there is no mention of the history of religions despite Barton's leadership of the group for many years. See Gordon, *Pennsylvania Tradition*, pp. 45-47.

75. The *1923-24 President's Report* stated, "During the year just closed, in harmony with the plan recommended by the faculty for cooperation with neighboring educational institutions in the field of History of Religions, Professor Royden K. Yerkes, through the courtesy of the faculty of the Philadelphia Divinity School, has given a two-hour course throughout the year. Arrangements have been made for the continuation of Professor Yerkes' services for another year; and a similar agreement has been entered into by the Crozer Theological Seminary whereby President Milton C. Evans will give a two-hour lecture course in this Department" (p. 25). Both Yerkes and Evans were listed in the university catalog as lecturers in the history of religions.

76. The first two post-Jastrow Ph.D.'s in the history of religions were awarded to Philadelphia pastors. Arthur C. James, pastor of St. Andrew's Methodist Episcopal Church, received his doctorate in 1925. His dissertation was titled "Taboo Among the Ancient Hebrews." John K. Shryock, assistant pastor at the Church of the Saviour, earned his Ph.D. in 1927 with the thesis "The Temples of Anking and Their Cults."

CHAPTER TWO

1. Veysey, *Emergence*, p. 12.

2. See ibid., chap. 5 for a discussion of the creation of the administrative apparatus of the new university.

3. Ibid., pp. 366-67.

4. Quoted in Thomas Wakefield Goodspeed, *A History of the University of Chicago: The First Quarter-Century* (Chicago: University of Chicago Press, 1916), p. 417.

5. Ibid., p. 401. It is significant that the most recent history of the early years of the University of Chicago by Richard J. Storr is titled *Harper's University: The Beginnings*.
6. The Baptist role in the founding of the University of Chicago is well documented. See Goodspeed, *A History of the University of Chicago*, pp. 1-97 and Richard J. Storr, *Harper's University: The Beginnings* (Chicago: University of Chicago Press, 1966), pp. 1-106. For an interesting account of Harper's relationship with Chicago Baptists, see Lars Hoffman, "William Rainey Harper and the Chicago Fellowship" (Ph.D. dissertation, University of Iowa, 1978).
7. William Rainey Harper, "The University and Democracy," *The Trend in Higher Education in America* (Chicago: University of Chicago Press, 1905), p. 3.
8. Ibid., p. 13.
9. William Rainey Harper, ed., *Religion and the Higher Life* (Chicago: University of Chicago Press, 1904), p. vii.
10. James Wind, "The Bible and the University: The Messianic Vision of William Rainey Harper" (Ph.D. dissertation, University of Chicago, 1983).
11. Ibid., p. 8.
12. Harper, *Higher Life*, p. 5.
13. Ibid., p. 13.
14. Ibid., p. 34.
15. Storr, *Harper's University*, p. 184.
16. Harper, *Trend*, p. 64.
17. Robert W. Lynn, "Notes Toward a History: Theological Encyclopedia and the Evolution of American Seminary Curriculum, 1808-1968," essay, The Lilly Endowment, Indianapolis, Ind., June 1979.
18. Harper, *Trend*, pp. 234-67.
19. Ibid., p. 236.
20. Ibid., p. 239.
21. Ibid., pp. 195-206.
22. Ibid., p. 198. Harper also displayed his practical side when he admitted, "I should like to propose the statement that the relative loss of influence of the minister is due to the smallness of his salary more than to all other influences combined" (p. 202).
23. Harper wrote six bulletins in the first seventeen months of his presidency that outlined his vision for the University of Chicago. *Official Bulletin No. 5* was published in March 1892 and presented Harper's thinking about the role of the divinity school. The six bulletins were published as *The University of Chicago Official Bulletins, 1891-92*.
24. *Official Bulletin No. 5* (Chicago: n.p., 1892), p. 6.
25. William Rainey Harper, *The President's Report, July 1892-July 1902* (Chicago: University of Chicago Press, 1903), p. lxxv. (Hereafter the *Decennial Report*.)
26. "Articles of Agreement Between the Baptist Theological Union, Located at Chicago, and the University of Chicago," *Official Bulletin No. 5*, pp. 3-6.

27. William Rainey Harper, "The Deluge in Other Literatures and History," *The Biblical World* 4 (August 1894): 123.
28. William Rainey Harper, "Editorial," *The Biblical World* 2 (1893): 241-46.
29. The strongest statement about Harper's relativist stance in regard to other religions is found in Cyrus Eaton's recollections of Harper and Rockefeller that were printed in the *University of Chicago Magazine*, May-June 1973. Eaton, an entrepreneur and Chicago trustee, worked for Rockefeller and in his youth had the occasion to meet Harper. In regard to religious matters Eaton wrote, "To Mr. Rockefeller and R. Harper, the most significant element of religion was the impetus it gave to the moral life, in encouraging men to do their duty to their families and their communities. I would be sure, from my knowledge of the two men, that they were both well aware that the religions people adopt, like the languages they speak, are accidents of birth." (p. 13).
30. Harper, "Editorial," *The Biblical World* 2 (1894): 245.
31. "Comparative Religion Notes," *The Biblical World* 8 (1896): 168.
32. Goodspeed to Harper, December 13, 1891, William Rainey Harper Papers, University of Chicago archives.
33. John Henry Barrows, "The Greatness of Religion," *Official Publications of the University of Chicago: The Quarterly Calendar* (Chicago: University of Chicago Press, 1894), p. 5.
34. The standard works of Harvard institutional history that cover the Eliot years are Samuel Eliot Morrison, ed., *The Development of Harvard University Since the Inauguration of President Eliot, 1869-1929* (Cambridge: Harvard University Press, 1930) and idem, *Three Centuries of Harvard, 1636-1936* (Cambridge: Harvard University Press, 1936). See also Hugh Hawkins, *Between Harvard and America: The Educational Leadership of Charles W. Eliot* (New York: University Press, 1972).
35. Quoted in Henry H. Saunderson, *Charles W. Eliot: Puritan Liberal* (New York: Harper & Bros., Publishers, 1928), pp. 10-11.
36. The American Unitarian Association was founded in Boston in 1825.
37. See Saunderson, *Puritan Liberal*, p. 92-102.
38. Henry James, *Charles W. Eliot: President of Harvard University, 1869-1909* (Boston: Houghton Mifflin Co., 1930), p. 302.
39. Charles W. Eliot, "The Crying Need of a Renewed Christianity," *A Late Harvest: Miscellaneous Papers Written Between Eighty and Ninety* (Boston: Atlantic Monthly Press, 1924), p. 231. (Italics mine.)
40. In William A. Neilson, ed., *Charles W. Eliot: The Man and His Beliefs*, 2 vols. (New York: Harper & Bros., 1926), 2:576-603.
41. *The New York Times* referred to Eliot's religion as "Pragmatic Pantheism." For this and other criticism by the religious world see Edward H. Cotton, *The Life of Charles W. Eliot* (Boston: Small, Maynard & Co., 1926), pp. 294-97.
42. Quoted in Cotton, *Life of Charles W. Eliot*, p. 289.
43. Ibid., p. 293.

44. Charles W. Eliot, *Annual Reports of the President and Treasurer of Harvard College, 1877-78* (Cambridge: Press of John Wilson & Son, 1879), p. 36.
45. To cite one example, in "The Religion of the Future," Eliot wrote, "The younger generations listen with incredulous smiles to the objection made only a little more than sixty years ago by some divines of the Scottish Presbyterian Church to the employment of chloroform in childbirth, namely, that the physicians were interfering with the execution of a curse pronounced by the Almighty," see Cotton, *Life of Charles W. Eliot*, p. 291.
46. James, *Charles W. Eliot*, p. 318.
47. Neilson, *Charles W. Eliot*, p. 8. (Italics mine.)
48. Charles W. Eliot, ed., "Address at the Inauguration of Daniel C. Gilman," *Educational Reform: Essays and Addresses* (New York: Century Co., 1909), p. 43.
49. Charles W. Eliot, "On the Education of Ministers," ibid., pp. 61-86.
50. Ibid., p. 70.
51. Ibid., p. 75.
52. *Annual Reports, 1874-75* (Harvard), p. 22.
53. This practice was discontinued in 1895 when tuition rates for divinity school students were raised to equal the rates of the other professional schools.
54. Hawkins, *Between Harvard and America*, p. 132.
55. *Annual Reports, 1878-79* (Harvard), pp. 24-25.
56. Ibid., *1900-1901*, p. 63.
57. Ibid., *1878-79*, p. 22.
58. Ibid., *1892-93*, p. 29.

CHAPTER THREE

1. The six were: Columbia, 6,232; Harvard, 5,558; Chicago, 5,487; Michigan, 5,259; Pennsylvania, 5,033; Cornell, 5,028. See Edwin E. Slosson, *Great American Universities* (New York: Macmillan Co., 1910), p. 475.
2. Harper claimed that in the major Protestant denominations between 1894 and 1904 there had been a 15 percent decrease in student enrollment. See his "Why Are There Fewer Students for the Ministry?" *The Trend*, pp. 195-206.
3. Goodspeed to Harper, April 14, 1892, President's Papers: 1889-1925, University of Chicago archives.
4. *President's Report, 1897-98* (Chicago), p. 37.
5. Ibid., *1899-1900*, p. xv.
6. Goodspeed to Harper, November 17, 1894, President's Papers: 1889-1925, University of Chicago archives.
7. *Decennial Report*, p. 29.
8. By way of example, the Department of History awarded 185 Ph.D.'s in the first twenty-four years of the university. For a comparison of all departments, see *President's Report, 1915-16* (Chicago), pp. 191-92.

9. The sources are: *Who's Who in America, 1903-1905*, s.v. "Buckley, Edmund"; correspondence related to his position at Chicago between 1894 and 1900 in the University of Chicago archives; a number of published works; and questionnaire data from the University of Michigan Alumni Records Office.

10. Goodspeed to Harper, July 15, 1894, President's Papers: 1889-1925, University of Chicago archives.

11. Edmund Buckley, "Die Mongolen" (pp. 43-49), "Die Chinesen" (pp. 50-77), "Die Japaner" (pp. 78-87), in *Lehrbuch der Religionsgeschichte*, ed. P. D. Chantepie de la Saussaye (Freiburg: J. C. B. Mohr, 1897).

12. Edmund Buckley, ed., *Universal Religion* (Chicago: University Association, 1897). The University Association was an outgrowth of the Columbian Exposition devoted to providing courses of study generally not available to the public.

13. For a listing of Buckley's publications, see "The General Index to Volumes I-XXVIII," *The Biblical World* 28 (1906): 438.

14. Buckley to Goodspeed, May 19, 1900, Divinity School Correspondence, University of Chicago archives.

15. The Mudlavia Sanitarium was a most curious choice by Buckley. It was essentially a health resort specializing in mud baths for the wealthy of America who were afflicted with arthritis, rheumatism, and related diseases. A short, unpublished history of Mudlavia depicts a luxury health spa catering to hundreds of people. Medical examinations and treatments were standard procedure but no reference is made to religious or educational programs. Although he labeled himself a lecturer in his 1918 letter to President Judson at Chicago, perhaps Buckley was more honest when, in a 1920 University of Michigan alumni survey, he listed his occupation as "social manager at Mudlavia Sanitarium."

16. Buckley to Judson, December 22, 1918, President's Papers: 1899-1925, University of Chicago archives.

17. Laetitia Moon Conard, "Leon Marillier," *The Open Court* 16 (1902): 50.

18. Laetitia Moon Conard, "A Visit to Quinault Indian Graves," *The Open Court* 19 (1905): 737-44.

19. Much of the biographical information on Laetitia Moon Conard was obtained in a telephone interview with her daughter, Rebecca French, of Grinnell, Iowa, on October 22, 1987.

20. The Grinnell College student newspaper, *Scarlet and Black*, on January 18, 1913, announced a course on the history of religion to be offered by Mrs. H. S. Conard during the spring semester, 1913. The college catalog for that year did not, however, list the course and it is not known whether the course was given. No other Religionswissenschaft courses, according to the college catalog, were offered by Laetitia Moon Conard during her tenure at Grinnell.

21. The two articles were: "Some Effects of the Depression on Family Life," *Social Forces* 15 (October 1936): 76-81 and "Differential Depression Effects on Families of Laborers, Farmers, and the Business Class," *American Journal of Sociology* 44 (January 1939): 526-33.

22. See Storr, *Harper's University*, pp. 129-31.

23. For degree requirements in the Department of Comparative Religion, see *University of Chicago Annual Registers, 1892-1900*.
24. *Annual Register, 1915-16* (Chicago), p. 141.
25. *Decennial Report*, p. 180.
26. The next highest enrollment was 88 students in the Department of Education. See *President's Report, 1916-17* (Chicago), p. 224.
27. Ibid., *1907-1908*, p. 15.
28. In a 1923 "Report on the Present Needs of the Graduate School of Arts and Literature," apparently authored by Chicago Dean Laing, the recommendation was made to promote Professor Haydon and give him some assistance. By doing so, the "weak" department (Comparative Religion), which "is chiefly the work of one man" (Haydon), "will be strengthened." President's Papers: 1889-1925, University of Chicago archives.
29. Charles W. Eliot, "More Harvard Graduates for the Ministry," *The Ministry as Profession: Three Addresses Delivered Before the Divinity Club of Harvard Divinity School* (Cambridge: Harvard Divinity School, 1907).
30. *Report of Overseers of Harvard College to Visit the Divinity School* (Cambridge: Harvard University Press, 1913).
31. Ibid., April 1934.
32. *Annual Reports, 1894-95* (Harvard), p. 24.
33. Ibid., *1906-07*, p. 145.
34. Ibid.
35. The thirty-one students enrolled in 1925-26 do not include those whose registration was in the affiliated institutions of the Episcopal Theological Seminary, Boston University School of Theology, or the Newton School of Theology.
36. The proportion of resident graduate students as a percentage of total enrollment in ten-year periods from 1890 to 1920 is as follows: 1890, 37%; 1900, 32%; 1910, 35%; 1920, 65%.
37. *Annual Reports, 1891-92* (Harvard), p. 24.
38. Levering Reynolds, Jr., "The Later Years: 1880-1953," in *Harvard Divinity School: Its Place in Harvard University*, ed. George Hunston Williams (Boston: Beacon Press, 1954), p. 188.
39. *Annual Reports, 1890-91* (Harvard), p. 99.
40. Ibid., *1894-95*, p. 136.
41. Some examples of Riale's publications are: "Why So Many Definitions of Religion?" *Popular Science Monthly* 37 (May-October 1890): 348-51; "The World's Religions at the World's Fair," *The Arena* 6 (June-November 1892): 243-49; "A New Analogy for Religious Experience," *The Biblical World* 17 (1898): 439-42; "Value and Danger of the Study of Comparative Religion," *The Biblical World* 4 (1894): 14-19.
42. F. N. Riale to Eliot, November 24, 1896, Eliot Papers, Harvard University archives.

43. Not surprisingly for a Presbyterian minister, Riale held that Christianity was the supreme religion. See his article, "The World's Religions at the World's Fair."

44. Although I have been unable to uncover the subsequent career of Pfatteicher, it is interesting to note that Brunner returned to Germany to teach systematic theology at Geissen University and Pyatt, after a brief stint as pastor of the Central Christian Church in Gary, Indiana, was appointed in 1920 as professor of Old Testament at the College of the Bible in Lexington, Kentucky.

45. *Annual Reports, 1889-90* (Harvard), p. 119.

46. Ibid., *1902-1903*, p. 29.

47. Harvard Divinity School, Minutes of Faculty Meetings, 1893-1912, meeting of October 28, 1902, Harvard University archives.

CHAPTER FOUR

1. The most important works in regard to the social sciences are: Mary O. Furner, *Advocacy and Objectivity: A Crisis in the Professionalization of American Social Science, 1865-1905* (Lexington: University Press of Kentucky, 1975) and Thomas Haskell, *The Emergence of Professional Social Science: The American Social Science Association and the Nineteenth Century Crisis of Authority* (Urbana: University of Illinois Press, 1977). Bruce Kuklick examines the professionalization of the Harvard philosophy faculty between 1860 and 1930 in *The Rise of American Philosophy* (New Haven: Yale University Press, 1977).

2. Edward Everett Hale, ed., *James Freeman Clarke: Autobiography, Diary and Correspondence* (Boston: Houghton Mifflin Co., 1891), p. 40.

3. James Freeman Clarke, *Ten Great Religions*, Vol. 1: *An Essay in Comparative Theology* (Boston: James R. Osgood & Co., 1871), p. 3.

4. Ibid.

5. James Freeman Clarke, *Ten Great Religions*, Vol. 2: *A Comparison of All Religions* (Boston: Houghton Mifflin & Co., 1888), pp. 4, 5.

6. In 1867-68 he was present two days per week; the following years only one day.

7. See Sydney Ahlstrom, "The Middle Period: 1840-80," in *The Harvard Divinity School*, ed. Williams, p. 113.

8. Ibid., p. 105. Prescribed reading for the bachelor of divinity examination at Harvard in 1869 included Maurice's *Religions of the World*.

9. The constitution of the Board of Overseers stipulated that a person who had served for two terms could not be reelected for a third term without a year's interval. Thus Clarke was selected to serve in 1866, 1873, 1880, and 1886.

10. Hale, *Clarke: Autobiography*, p. 296.

11. Ibid., p. 299.

12. Charles Carroll Everett, *The Science of Thought* (Boston: DeWolf, Fiske & Co., 1869).

13. Crawford Howell Toy, "Charles Carroll Everett," *The New World* 9 (1900): 714-24.

14. Charles Carroll Everett, *Theism and the Christian Faith*, ed. Edward Hale (New York: Macmillan Co., 1909), p. 489.
15. Everett's lecture "The Psychological Basis of Religious Faith" was originally titled "The Science of Religion." His decision to drop the phrase was no doubt related to his argument that in religion and theology there is, unlike in science, no universal agreement as to what should be studied. Furthermore, in science all things are of equal value whereas "the study of religion involves judgments of value." Everett concluded that "we speak more properly of a philosophy of religion than of a science of religion." See Charles Carroll Everett, *The Psychological Elements of Religious Faith*, ed. Edward Hale (New York: Macmillan Co., 1902), pp. 6-8.
16. This course is variously referred to as Everett's lectures on East Asiatic religions, history of religions, and historical religions. Furthermore, some accounts claim Everett offered two courses during his tenure (one on theology proper and one on the East Asiatic religions) and others suggest there were three courses, the psychological roots of religion, historical religions, and philosophy of religion.
17. Toy, "Charles Carroll Everett," p. 720.
18. Everett's only book on the history of religions was *Religions Before Christianity* (1883). His use and treatment of eastern religions, although less prominent, also shows through in *Poetry, Comedy and Duty* (1888) and *The Psychological Elements of Religious Faith* (1902).
19. William Fenn, "The Theological School: 1869-1928," in *Development of Harvard*, ed. Morrison, p. 470. Everett himself made the same point in his annual report of 1880-81: "The Bussey Professor will retain the departments of Systematic Theology and Comparative Religion. These two studies are closely connected and it is helpful to have both in the same hands" (p. 65).
20. During the nine years of *The New World*'s existence, 1892-1900, an amazing array of articles with Religionswissenschaft themes appeared from the pens of scholars. A brief sample includes: "The Foundation of Buddhism" by Maurice Bloomfield (1892); "The Role of the History of Religions in Education" by Jean Reville (1892); "The Parliament of Religions" by C. H. Toy (1893); "The Shinto Pantheon" by Edmund Buckley (1896); "Some Aspects of Islam" by Albert Reville (1897).
21. Everett wrote and published eight articles for *The New World*. They were: "The Historic and the Ideal Christ" (1892); "Tennyson and Browning as Scriptural Forces" (1893); "The Devil" (1895); "Paul's Doctrine of the Atonement" (1896); "Kant's Influence in Theology" and "Reason in Religion" (1897); "Beyond Good and Evil" (1898); and "The Distinctive Mark of Christianity" (1899).
22. Eliot to Everett, September 18, 1900, Eliot Papers, Harvard University archives.
23. Toy's metamorphosis in regard to the infallibility of Scripture is outlined in John A. Broadus, *Memoir of James Petigru Boyce* (New York: A. C. Armstrong & Son, 1893) and summarized in David G. Lyon's "Crawford Howell Toy," *Harvard Theological Review* 13 (January 1920): 1-22 and George Foot Moore's "An Appreciation of Professor Toy," *The American Journal of Semitic Languages and*

Literatures 36 (October 1919): 1-7. Moore gives much more importance to Toy's strong interest in natural science than his acquaintance with the views of Wellhausen and Darwin.

24. A bibliography of Toy's works, prepared by Harry Wolfson, appears in *Studies in the History of Religions*, ed. David G. Lyon and George Foot Moore (New York: Macmillan Co., 1912), pp. 367-73.

25. *Annual Reports, 1879-80* (Harvard), p. 31.

26. Moore, "An Appreciation," pp. 5-6.

27. David Gordon Lyon, himself a member of the club, described it as follows: "This Club comprises a small group of Harvard instructors and an occasional member from the outside. Dr. Toy's chief interest during the later years of his life was the broad field of religion, and he was rarely happier than in the monthly meetings of this group of congenial friends." Lyon, "Crawford Howell Toy," p. 18.

28. The Harvard archives contain a folder on the History of Religions Club. Unfortunately, the material is sketchy and it is very difficult to determine the exact membership of the group in any given year. Nevertheless, there is a copy of a poem read at the March 3, 1906 meeting. The faculty in attendance for that meeting consisted of: Putnam (anthropology); Newell (medicine); C. R. Lanman (ancient languages); G. F. Moore (divinity); Sheldon (philology); D. G. Lyon (divinity); Kittredge (English); C. H. Toy (divinity); F. N. Robinson (English); R. B. Dixon (anthropology); J. H. Wright (Greek), C. H. Moore (Latin); G. A. Reisner (archaeology). After Toy's retirement, C. R. Lanman took over the leadership of the club.

29. Crawford Howell Toy, "The Parliament of Religions," *The New World* 2 (1893): 739-40.

30. The reviews appeared in the 1892, 1896, and 1898 issues respectively.

31. Crawford Howell Toy, *Introduction to the History of Religions* (Boston: Ginn & Co., 1913), p. vii.

32. See Toy's "Taboo and Morality" 20 (1899): 151-56; "Relation Between Magic and Religion" 20 (1899): 327-31; and "Recent Discussions of Totemism" 25 (1904): 146-61, in the *Journal of the American Oriental Society*.

33. Earl Boynton Wood, "Annual Report of 1894-95," History of Harvard Divinity School—Student Annual Reports, Harvard University archives.

34. G. F. Moore to Eliot, May 30, 1901, Eliot Papers, Harvard University archives. Toy had one month earlier strongly recommended Moore to Eliot. "In regard to Professor G. F. Moore I have to say that I think he would be a great addition to our force, and I should be very glad to see him in the Harvard Faculty. . . . I regard him as one of the ablest men in this country." Toy to Eliot, May 1, 1901, Eliot Papers, Harvard University archives.

35. The Frothingham family were long and generous supporters of the divinity school. Paul Frothingham was appointed to the committee to visit the divinity school by the Board of Governors. The family did not have a special interest in the history of religions. The decision to give the Frothingham professorship to Moore was Eliot's and Fenn's.

36. Edward Caldwell Moore, "Notes in Memorial of George Foot Moore, Frothingham Professor of the History of Religions in Harvard University," typewritten paper, May 1931, Harvard University archives.
37. *Annual Reports, 1901-1902* (Harvard), p. 171. Unfortunately, I was unable to find any other administrative or academic association of Moore with the seven other teachers. The only possibility, albeit very speculative, was found in the course listing in the university catalog for 1902-1903. There, under courses of instruction in the history of religions, graduate students were directed to seven other university courses and six other professors for related work. The other courses and professors were: Religions of India, Charles R. Lanman; the Religion and Worship of the Greeks, Clifford H. Moore; Greek Mythology, Charles B. Gulick; Primitive Religions, Dixon; History of Christian Thought, to the Eighteenth Century, Ephraim Emerton; History of Christian Thought Since Kant, Edmund C. Moore. George Foot Moore's The Hebrew Religion was the seventh course listed. See *Catalogue, 1902-1903* (Harvard), p. 383.
38. Fenn, "The Theological School: 1869-1928," p. 470.
39. E. C. Moore, "Note in Memorial," p. 5.
40. William Wallace Fenn, "George Foot Moore: A Memoir," *Proceedings of the Massachusetts Historical Society* 64 (October 1930-June 1932): 428.
41. E. C. Moore, "Note in Memorial," p. 1.
42. Fenn, "George Foot Moore," p. 428.
43. Examples in the *Harvard Theological Review* are Moore's "Intermediaries in Jewish Theology" 15 (1922): 41-95; "The Covenanteers of Damascus, a Hitherto Unknown Jewish Sect" 4 (1911): 330-77; "A Jewish Life of Jesus" 16 (1923): 93-103; "The Rise of Normative Judaism. II. to the Close of the Misnah" 18 (1925): 1-38.
44. Fenn, "George Foot Moore," p. 429. Moore published two other books between 1902 and his death in 1931. The first, *The Literature of the Old Testament* (1913), illustrated his continued interest in the Old Testament after his Harvard appointment. The second, *The Birth and Growth of Religion* (1923), did not indicate Moore's widening fascination for the history of religions generally. Edward Caldwell Moore referred to his brother's lack of enthusiasm for the topic of the book. The book was written from lectures given at Union Theological Seminary in New York solely because of the popularity of the issue of the origins of religions. See E. C. Moore, "Note in Memorial," p. 7.
45. E. C. Moore, "Note in Memorial,", p. 7.
46. George Foot Moore, *History of Religions*, 2 vols. (New York: Charles Scribner's Sons, 1948), 1:vii.
47. George Foot Moore, review of *Comparative Religion*, by F. B. Jevons, in *Harvard Theological Review* 7 (1914): 611.
48. George Foot Moore, review of *Comparative Religion: Its Adjuncts and Allies*, by Louis H. Jordan, in *Harvard Theological Review* 9 (1916): 431.
49. E. C. Moore, "Note in Memorial," pp. 4, 8.
50. George Foot Moore, "The Field of an Undenominational School of Theology," *Harvard Graduates Magazine* 11 (1902): 204.

51. Ibid., p. 206.
52. W. H. P. Faunce to Harper, January 16, 1888, President's Papers: 1889-1925, University of Chicago archives.
53. Thomas Wakefield Goodspeed, the uncle of George S. Goodspeed, referred to the special friendship of George Goodspeed and Harper. "But considerate and unassertive though he [Harper] always was, with most of his friends he was still necessarily the President. There were a few very intimate ones—they might almost be called his cronies—with whom he could unbend and be entirely at his ease. Such men were Mr. Herman A. Kohlsaat, the editor of the *Chicago Inter-Ocean*, Major Henry A. Rust, the University Comptroller, Rev. Wallace Buttrick, afterward chairman of the General Education Board, Professor George S. Goodspeed, and Dean Eri B. Hulbert of the Divinity School." Thomas W. Goodspeed, *William Rainey Harper* (Chicago: University of Chicago Press, 1928), p. 161.
54. "The Life and Times of Christ, Based on Luke" and "The Gospel of John: Jesus Manifested as the Son of God" were coauthored by Goodspeed and Harper and copyrighted in 1890 and 1891 respectively by the American Institute of Sacred Literature.
55. George Stephen Goodspeed, "The Twenty-Fourth Psalm: An Expository Sketch," *The Old and New Testament Student* 9 (1889): 329-35; idem, "The Proverbs of the Bible and Other Proverbs," *The Old and New Testament Student* 13 (1891): 344-48.
56. Goodspeed had spoken with Harper about the opportunity in Chicago while the two men were at Yale. On May 26, 1890, George Goodspeed wrote to his uncle Thomas Wakefield Goodspeed, a man who later played a significant administrative role at the University of Chicago as secretary of the Board of Trustees, "Last evening I had a long talk with him [Harper] about Chicago matters which it seemed to me might be strictly confidential as it would not do for him to know that I had written you. I found to my great surprise that he was quite favorably inclined to Chicago. . . . I know that he has even gone so far as to formulate clearly certain conditions on which he would go if asked." President's Papers: 1889-1925, University of Chicago archives.
57. Ibid., November 8, 1891.
58. Goodspeed to Harper, November 29, 1891, William Rainey Harper Papers, University of Chicago archives.
59. Goodspeed to Harper, February 14, 1892, President's Papers: 1889-1925, University of Chicago archives.
60. Goodspeed to Harper, April 14, 1892, Harper Papers, University of Chicago archives.
61. Although open to "prepared" college students, Goodspeed's courses in the Department of Comparative Religion and the Department of Semitic Languages and Literatures were intended primarily for graduate and divinity students.
62. Edmund Buckley's two articles were: "On the Need of Systematic Study of Religion," *The Biblical World* 3 (1894): 119-27; "A Sketch of the Science of Religion," *The Biblical World* 23 (1904): 256-62, 349-57.

63. For a listing of Goodspeed's articles published in *The Biblical World*, see "The General Index to Volumes I-XXVIII," *The Biblical World* 28 (1906): 443.
64. "Comparative Religion Notes," *The Biblical World* 2 (1894): 131.
65. George Stephen Goodspeed, "Editorial," *The Biblical World* 6 (1895): 326.
66. Mary Eleanor Barrows, *John Henry Barrows: A Memoir* (Chicago: Fleming H. Revell Co., 1904), p. 301.
67. Caroline Haskell, a parishioner of John H. Barrows, endowed two lectureships at Chicago on comparative religion. The first, the Haskell Lectures, was endowed in April 1894 and the Barrows lectureship was created in October of the same year to be given in India. Both were for the purpose of comparing Christianity to other religions.
68. "George Stephen Goodspeed," *The Biblical World* 25 (1905): 169-72.
69. Goodspeed to Harper, January 3, 1905, President's Papers: 1889-1925, University of Chicago archives.
70. Foster to Harper, January 25, 1905, ibid.
71. *President's Annual Report, 1904-1905* (Chicago), p. 47.
72. Walker to Harper, November 10, 1904, Divinity School Correspondence, University of Chicago archives.
73. For a summation of the Foster controversy, see Alan Wayne Gragg, "Formative Influences on the Development of the Religious Humanism of George Burman Foster" (Ph.D. dissertation, Duke University, 1961), pp. 78-85.
74. Hulbert to Rev. C. D. Mayhew, March 27, 1906, Divinity School Correspondence, University of Chicago archives.
75. Quoted in J. V. Nash, "A Twentieth Century Emancipator,'" *The Open Court* 36 (June 1922): 330.
76. See Gragg, "Formative Influence," p. 234.
77. Alan W. Gragg, *George Burman Foster: Religious Humanist* (Danville, Va.: Association of Baptist Professors of Religion, 1978), p. 234.
78. James Hayden Tufts, "George Burman Foster," *The University Record* (Chicago: University of Chicago Press) 5 (1919): 182.
79. For a complete bibliography of Foster, see Gragg, "Formative Influences," pp. 238-47.
80. Foster's five reviews were: *Die Aufgabe der theologischen Facultäten und die allgemeine Religionsgeschichte*, by Adolf Harnack, *The American Journal of Theology* 7 (April 1903): 332-35; *The Evolution of Religion*, by L. R. Farnell, *The American Journal of Theology* 12 (April 1908): 324-25; *Religion and Historic Faiths*, by Otto Pfleiderer, *The American Journal of Theology* 12 (April 1908): 323-24; *The Religion of the Veda*, by Maurice Bloomfield, *The American Journal of Theology* 13 (April 1909): 308-9; *The Systems of the Vedanta According to Badarayana G. Brahma-Suytras and Cankara's Commentary*, by Paul Deussen, *The American Journal of Theology* 14 (April 1915): 300.
81. Foster titled his book review of Harnack's *Die Aufgabe der theologischen Facultäten und die allgemeine Religionsgeschichte* "Comparative Religion and the Theological Curriculum." He disagreed strongly with Harnack's proposal that the

theological faculty of a university should concern itself only with the investigation and exposition of Christianity. He argued that Christianity and other religions must be studied historically; all had gone through an evolutionary process of development. See *The American Journal of Theology* 7 (April 1903): 332-35.

82. Shailer Mathews, *New Faith for Old: An Autobiography* (New York: Macmillan Co., 1936), p. 69.

83. William Wallace Fenn, "Professor Foster as a Theologian," *The University Record* 5 (1919): 177.

84. Tufts, "Foster," p. 181.

85. Divinity School Faculty Minutes, Meeting of January 11, 1919, University of Chicago archives.

86. It may be safely assumed that there was some discussion regarding the transfer of the work of the Department of Comparative Religion to the divinity school. Unfortunately, I have been unable to discover a specific recommendation or plan by the divinity faculty.

87. J. S. Dickerson to A. Eustace Haydon, January 15, 1919, Personal Files of A. Eustace Haydon, in possession of Ethel Haydon, Pacific Palisades, California.

88. Both of Haydon's letters of appointment, dated May 15, 1919, and August 20, 1920, are in the possession of Ethel Haydon.

89. George Burman Foster, *Friedrich Nietzsche*, ed. Curtis W. Reese, with an Introduction by A. Eustace Haydon (New York: Macmillan Co., 1931), p. ix.

90. Haydon wrote or edited five books during his twenty-six years at Chicago. They were: *The Quest of Ages* (1929), *Modern Trends in World Religions* (1934), *The Heritage of Eastern Asia* (1932), *Man's Search for the Good Life* (1937), and *Biography of the Gods* (1941). Among his most relevant articles for the history of religion were: "From Comparative Religion to History of Religions," *Journal of Religion* 2 (1922): 577-89; "Twenty-Five Years of History of Religions," *Journal of Religion* 6 (1926): 17-40; "What Constitutes a Scientific Interpretation of Religion?" *Journal of Religion* 6 (1926): 234-49; "Science of Religion," *A Dictionary of Religion and Ethics*, ed. Shailer Mathews and Gerald Birney Smith (New York: Macmillan Co., 1921), p. 402. The complete biography and bibliography of Haydon are with his papers in the possession of Ethel Haydon.

91. From 1919 to 1930 the Department of Comparative Religion awarded six Ph.D.'s and eight M.A.'s.

CHAPTER FIVE

1. William Rainey Harper, "The Trend of University and College Education in the United States," *The North American Review*, April 1902, p. 459.

2. *Decennial Report*, p. lxxiv.

3. Mathews, *New Faith for Old*, p. 59.

4. Mathews to Harper, September 29, 1905, Divinity School Correspondence, University of Chicago archives.
5. Mathews to Burton, January 12, 1925, Divinity School Correspondence, University of Chicago archives.
6. *Decennial Report*, p. 199.
7. The tremendous increase in the number of master of arts degrees awarded in the divinity school between 1893 and 1920 somewhat skews the percentage drop. If we simply compare D.B.'s with Ph.D.'s, the decrease in the percentage of D.B.'s awarded is from 96 percent (1897) to 76 percent (1906) to 73 (1915). Nevertheless, between 1910 and 1919 118 bachelor's degrees were conferred and 49 doctorates were given, indicating a significant interest in graduate studies. See *President's Report, 1917-19* (Chicago), p. 316.
8. Ibid., *1913-14*, p. 52.
9. Graduate theses accepted between 1917 and 1919 with Religionswissenschaft topics included: "The Relation Between Religion and Science: A Biological Approach," "Social Influences in the Development of Mohammedanism," "The 'Way of Salvation' in the Ramayana of the Tulsi Dass," and "Indications of Primitive Chinese Religion in the Confucian Classics."
10. Mathews to Judson, January 22, 1919, Divinity School Correspondence, University of Chicago archives.
11. *President's Report, 1927-28* (Chicago), pp. 9-10.
12. "Comparative Religion Notes," *The Biblical World* 4 (1894): 293.
13. Divinity School, Minutes of Faculty Meetings, 1904-1913, University of Chicago archives.
14. Mathews to Swazey, December 30, 1915, Divinity School Correspondence, University of Chicago archives.
15. Mathews to Judson memorandum, January 22, 1919, ibid.
16. *The President's Report, 1923-24* (Chicago), p. 13.
17. Ibid., *1921-22*, p. 10.
18. Robert Kelly, "The University of Chicago Divinity School," paper, November 11, 1924, Divinity School Correspondence, University of Chicago archives.
19. Mathews to Judson, October 21, 1920, ibid.
20. Between 1925 and 1930, five students received doctorates in comparative religion. Of the five, one went to India as assistant principal of a missionary college in Lucknow, and one returned as a missionary to Kobe, Japan.
21. Moore, "Field of an Undenominational School," p. 201. (Italics mine.)
22. I have been unable to locate any other statement in which Moore explicitly discussed the purpose and significance of the history of religions for seminary or university students.
23. *Annual Reports, 1915-16* (Harvard), p. 21.
24. Williams, *Harvard Divinity School*, p. 10.
25. Edward Caldwell Moore served as Parkman Professor of Theology at Harvard until 1915, when he became the Plummer Professor of Christian Morals and chairman of the Board of Preachers. His nonevangelical interest in Christian missions arose from his love for Reformation and post-Reformation church

history and was centered administratively in his position as president of the American Board of Commissioners for Foreign Missions from 1914 to 1923. He published two books of interest to missions work, *The Spread of Christianity in the Modern World* (1919) and *West and East* (1920).

26. The 1913 overseers suggested that "the prime desideratum of the School at the present moment is the appointment of one or more full professors in these subjects [homiletics, pastoral care, and religious education], who shall bring their ministerial experience, zeal and enthusiasm to inform and inspire the School." *Report of the Overseers of Harvard College: Committee to Visit the Divinity School, 1913,* n.p., Harvard University archives.

27. Reynolds, "Later Years," p. 215.

28. Willard L. Sperry, "Preparation for the Ministry in a Non-Denominational School," in *Harvard Divinity School,* ed. Williams, pp. 284-85.

29. The faculty minutes of March 31, 1896 were indicative of this problem. After discussion regarding the divinity faculty's role in registering Ph.D. candidates, it was "voted, to authorize the Dean to consider and decide in connection with the Dean of the Graduate School doubtful cases of registration." Harvard Divinity School, Minutes of Faculty Meetings, 1893-1912, Harvard University archives.

30. H. H. Horne, "Annual Report of 1898-99," History of Harvard Divinity School, Harvard University archives.

31. Fenn to Mathews, March 23, 1909, Divinity School Correspondence, University of Chicago archives.

32. *Annual Reports, 1901-1902* (Harvard), p. 171.

33. Ibid., *1911-12,* p. 127.

34. Ibid., *1914-15,* p. 139.

35. Divinity School, Minutes of Faculty Meetings, 1912-22, Harvard University archives.

36. In the case of Charles Lynn Pyatt, the faculty minutes of June 17, 1916 record that he received his Th.D. "on the ground of studies in the field of the History of Religions." A November 1, 1916 letter from the divinity faculty to divinity school alumni, however, listed Pyatt's field as Old Testament. As mentioned, Pyatt later became professor of Old Testament at the College of the Bible in Lexington, Kentucky.

    The *1922 Harvard University Catalogue* listed Carl Friedrich Pfatteicher as having received his Th.D. in the history and philosophy of religion. The faculty minutes of June 19, 1922, however, claim he was awarded his higher degree in theology.

37. *Annual Reports, 1928-29* (Harvard), p. 173.

38. Ibid., p. 175.

39. Ibid.

CHAPTER SIX

1. Jordan, *Comparative Religion: Its Recent Literature*, p. 3.
2. Jastrow, "Historical Study of Religions," p. 324.
3. E. C. Moore, "Note in Memorial," p. 5.
4. George A. Gordon, untitled address, in *First Quarter Centennial of Boston University: Program and Addresses* (Boston: Riverdale Press, 1898), p. 55.
5. Bishop Doane, untitled address, in *Proceedings and Addresses at the Twenty-Fifth Anniversary of the Opening of Cornell University* (Ithaca: Cornell University Press, 1893), p. 101.
6. In 1922 Chicago's Albert Eustace Haydon wrote an article for *The Journal of Religion*, in which he argued that the history of religions needed to take into account the tremendous variety and individuality of the world's religions. Comparative religion scholars had often erred by doing apologetics under the guise of scientific research. The science of religion had often, unfortunately, meant no abandonment of the traditional theory of divine revelation. Such theories "are apologetics and should be frankly so named. Scholars who have been working to win a place for comparative religion among the empirical sciences have a just cause of complaint against this appropriation of the name." "From Comparative Religion to History of Religions."
7. Jastrow, "Historical Study of Religions," p. 320.
8. Mathews wrote in his autobiography in 1936, "Those of us who were young men in the last two decades of the nineteenth century will recall the zeal with which men turned to the study of Hebrew. The interest was not merely literary or historical. It was really born of the evangelical belief in the Bible itself as the word of God." Mathews, *New Faith*, p. 61.
9. *Register of Doctors of Philosophy, June 1893-April 1938* (Chicago: University of Chicago Press, 1938).
10. In April 1896, Jastrow presented a plan for an "Association for the Historical Study of Religions" at the annual meeting of the American Oriental Society. The following year a special section of the AOS devoted to the historical study of religion was established and Jastrow was named secretary. In the ensuing years papers—often esoteric treatments of primitive or Oriental religions—were presented by members of the special section whose numbers never reached greater than thirty and by 1910 had dwindled to fourteen. In 1911, the directors of the AOS voted to discontinue the special section.

Bibliography

PRIMARY SOURCES

Books

Bishop, Morris. *A History of Cornell*. Ithaca: Cornell University Press, 1962.

Chamberlain, Joshua L., ed. *Universities and Their Sons: New York University*. Boston: R. Herdon Co., 1901.

Cheyney, Edward Potts. *History of the University of Pennsylvania: 1740-1940*. Philadelphia: University of Pennsylvania Press, 1940.

Clarke, James Freeman. *Ten Great Religions*. Vol. 1: *An Essay in Comparative Theology*. Boston: James R. Osgood & Co., 1871.

_____. *Ten Great Religions*. Vol. 2: *A Comparison of All Religions*. Boston: Houghton Mifflin Co., 1888.

Ellinwood, Mary G. *Frank Field Ellinwood*. New York: Fleming H. Revell Co., 1911.

Gordon, Cyrus H. *The Pennsylvania Tradition of Semitics*. Atlanta: Scholars Press, 1986.

Hale, Edward Everett, ed. *James Freeman Clarke: Autobiography, Diary and Correspondence*. Boston: Houghton Mifflin Co., 1891.

Harper, William Rainey. *The Trend in Higher Education in America*. Chicago: University of Chicago Press, 1905.

_____, ed. *Religion and the Higher Life*. Chicago: University of Chicago Press, 1904.

Hewett, Thomas. *Cornell University: A History*. 2 vols. New York: University Publishing Society, 1905.

Jastrow, Morris, Jr. *The Study of Religion*. London: W. Scott, 1901.

_____. "The Scope and Method of the Historical Study of Religions." In *Memoirs of the International Congress of Anthropology*. Edited by C. Staniland Wake. Chicago: Schulte Publishing Co., 1894.

Jones, Theodore F., ed. *New York University, 1832-1932*. New York: University Press, 1933.

Jordan, Louis H. *Comparative Religion: A Survey of Its Recent Literature*. London: Oxford University Press, 1910.

_____. *Comparative Religion: Its Adjuncts and Allies*. London: Oxford University Press, 1915.

_____. *Comparative Religion: Its Genesis and Growth*. Edinburgh: T. & T. Clark, 1905.

Kitagawa, Joseph. "The History of Religions in America." In *The History of Religions: Essays in Methodology*. Edited by Mircea Eliade and Joseph Kitagawa. Chicago: University of Chicago Press, 1959. Pp. 1-30.

Lyon, David G., and George Foot Moore, eds. *Studies in the History of Religions*. New York: Macmillan Co., 1912.

Moore, George Foot. *History of Religions*. 2 vols. New York: Charles Scribner's Sons, 1948.

Morrison, Samuel Eliot. *The Development of Harvard University Since the Inauguration of President Eliot, 1869-1929*. Cambridge: Harvard University Press, 1930.

_____. *Three Centuries of Harvard, 1636-1936*. Cambridge: Harvard University Press, 1936.

Oleson, Alexandra, and John Voss, eds. *The Organization of Knowledge in Modern America, 1860-1920*. Baltimore: Johns Hopkins University Press, 1979.

Oxtoby, Willard. "Religionswissenschaft Revisited." In *Religions in Antiquity, Essays in Memory of E. R. Goodenough*. Edited by Jacob Neusner. Vol. 14: *Studies in the History of Religions*. Leiden: E. J. Brill, 1968. Pp. 590-608.

Reville, Albert. *Prolegomena of the History of Religions*. Translated by A. S. Squire. London: Williams & Norgate, 1884.

Reynolds, Levering, Jr. "The Later Years: 1880-1953." In *Harvard Divinity School: Its Place in Harvard University*. Edited by George Hunston Williams. Boston: Beacon Press, 1954. Pp. 173-92.

Sharpe, Eric. *Comparative Religion: A History*. New York: Charles Scribner's Sons, 1975.

Tiele, Cornelius P. *Elements of the Science of Religion*. 2 vols. New York: Charles Scribner's Sons, 1869-99.

Toy, Crawford Howell. *Introduction to the History of Religions*. Boston: Ginn & Co., 1913.

Veysey, Laurence R. *The Emergence of the American University*. Chicago: University of Chicago Press, 1965.

Warren, William F. *The Religions of the World and the World-Religion*. New York: Eaton & Mains, 1911.

Welch, Claude. *Graduate Education in Religion*. Missoula: University of Montana Press, 1971.

_____. *Religion in the Undergraduate Curriculum: An Analysis and Interpretation*. Washington, D.C.: Association of American Colleges, 1971.

Articles

Buckley, Edmund. "On the Need of Systematic Study of Religion." *The Biblical World* 3 (1894): 119-27.

_____. "A Sketch of the Science of Religion." *The Biblical World* 23 (1904): 256-62.

"Comparative Religion Notes." *The Biblical World*. January-June 1894-1899.

Dictionary of American Biography. 1933 ed. S.v. "Morris Jastrow."

Fenn, William Wallace. "George Foot Moore: A Memoir." In *Proceedings of the Massachusetts Historical Society* 64 (October 1930-June 1932): 427-30.

_____. "Professor Foster as a Theologian." *The University of Chicago Record* 5 (1919): 175-78.

"George Stephen Goodspeed." *The Biblical World* 25 (1905): 169-72.

Goodenough, Erwin R. "Religionswissenschaft." *Numen* 6 (1959): 77-95.

Haydon, Albert Eustace. "From Comparative Religion to History of Religions." *Journal of Religion* 2 (1922): 577-89.

_____. "Twenty-Five Years of History of Religions." *Journal of Religion* 6 (1926): 17-40.

Jastrow, Morris, Jr. "The Historical Study of Religions at the University of Pennsylvania." *Old Penn*, March 11, 1911, pp. 644-45.

_____. "The Historical Study of Religions in Universities and Colleges." *The New World* 20 (1899): 309-22.

_____. "Recent Movements in the Historical Study of Religions in America." *The Biblical World* 1 (1893): 24-32.

Kitagawa, Joseph. "The 1893 World's Parliament of Religions and Its Legacy." Pamphlet printed by the University of Chicago Divinity School and the Baptist Theological Union, n.d.

Lyon, David G. "Crawford Howell Toy." *Harvard Theological Review* 13 (January 1920): 1-22.

Moore, Edward Caldwell. "Notes in Memorial of George Foot Moore, Frothingham Professor of the History of Religions in Harvard University." Typewritten paper, May 1931. Harvard University Archives.

Moore, George Foot. "An Appreciation of Professor Toy." *American Journal of Semitic Languages and Literatures* 36 (October 1919): 1-7.

_____. "The Field of an Undenominational School of Theology." *Harvard Graduates Magazine* 11 (1902): 202-9.

Reville, Jean. "The Role of the History of Religions in Modern Religious Education." *The New World* 1 (1892): 503-19.

Toy, Crawford Howell. "Charles Carroll Everett." *The New World* 9 (1900): 714-24.

Tufts, James Hayden. "George Burman Foster." *The University of Chicago Record* 5 (1919): 181-82.

SECONDARY SOURCES

Books

Ahlstrom, Sydney E. *A Religious History of the American People.* New Haven: Yale University Press, 1972.

Ault, Warren O. *Boston University: The College of Liberal Arts, 1873-1973.* Boston: Boston University Press, 1973.

Buckley, Edmund, ed. *Universal Religion.* Chicago: University Association, 1897.

Curti, Merle, ed. *American Scholarship in the Twentieth Century.* Cambridge: Harvard University Press, 1953.

de la Saussaye, P. D. Chantepie, ed. *Lehrbuch der Religionswissenschaft.* 2 vols. Freiburg: J. C. B. Mohr, 1897.

de Vries, Jan. *Perspectives in the History of Religions.* Translated by Kees W. Bolle. Berkeley: University of California Press, 1967.

Eliot, Charles W., ed. "More Harvard Graduates for the Ministry." In *The Ministry as Profession: Three Addresses Delivered Before the Divinity Club of Harvard Divinity School.* Cambridge: Harvard Divinity School, 1907.

Furner, Mary O. *Advocacy and Objectivity: A Crisis in the Professionalization of American Social Science, 1865-1905*. Lexington: University of Kentucky Press, 1975.

Goodspeed, Thomas Wakefield. *A History of the University of Chicago: The First Quarter Century*. Chicago: University of Chicago Press, 1916.

Gragg, Alan W. *George Burman Foster: Religious Humanist*. Danville, Va.: Association of Baptist Professors of Religion, 1978.

Haskell, Thomas. *The Emergence of Professional Social Science: The American Social Science Association and the Nineteenth Century Crisis of Authority*. Urbana: University of Illinois Press, 1977.

Hofstadter, Richard, and Walter Metzger. *The Development of Academic Freedom in the United States*. New York: Columbia University Press, 1955.

Hutchinson, William R. *The Modernist Impulse in American Protestantism*. Cambridge: Harvard University Press, 1976.

James, Henry. *Charles W. Eliot: President of Harvard University, 1869-1909*. Boston: Houghton Mifflin Co., 1930.

Jencks, Christopher, and David Reisman. *The Academic Revolution*. Garden City, N.Y.: Doubleday, 1968.

Kuklick, Bruce. *The Rise of American Philosophy*. New Haven: Yale University Press, 1977.

Mathews, Shailer. *New Faith for Old: An Autobiography*. New York: Macmillan Co., 1936.

Neilson, William A., ed. *Charles W. Eliot: The Man and His Beliefs*. 2 vols. New York: Harper & Bros., 1926.

Rudolph, Frederick. *The American College and University: A History*. New York: Random House, 1961.

Russett, Cynthia E. *Darwin in America: The Intellectual Response, 1865-1912*. San Francisco: W. H. Freeman & Co., 1976.

Storr, Richard J. *Harper's University: The Beginnings*. Chicago: University of Chicago Press, 1966.

Wind, James. "The Bible and the University: The Messianic Vision of William Rainey Harper." Ph.D. dissertation, University of Chicago, 1983.

Articles

Cameron, Richard Morgan. "Boston University, School of Theology: 1839-1968." *Nexus* 11 (May 1968): 34-52.

Conard, Laetitia Moon. "A Visit to the Quinault Indian Graves." *The Open Court* 19 (1905): 737-44.

Goodspeed, George Stephen. "The Proverbs of the Bible and Other Proverbs." *The Old and New Testament Student* 13 (1891): 344-48.

_____. "The Twenty-Fourth Psalm: A Expository Sketch." *The Old and New Testament Student* 9 (1889): 329-35.

Harper, William Rainey. "The Deluge in Other Literatures and History." *The Biblical World* 4 (August 1894): 118-26.

_____. "The Trend of University and College Education in the United States." *North American Review*, April 1902, pp. 452-61.

Haydon, Albert Eustace. "What Constitutes a Scientific Interpretation of Religion." *Journal of Religion* 6 (1926): 234-49.

Jastrow, Morris, Jr. "Cornelius Petrus Tiele." *The Independent* 54 (1902): 510-12.

_____. "Cornelius Petrus Tiele: In Commemoration of His Seventieth Birthday." *The Open Court* 14 (1900): 728-33.

Riale, Franklin N. "Value and Danger of the Study of Comparative Religion." *The Biblical World* 4 (1894): 14-19.

_____. "The World's Religions at the World's Fair." *The Arena* 6 (June-November 1892): 243-49.

Toy, Crawford Howell. "The Parliament of Religions." *The New World* 2 (1893): 739-40.

Newspapers

Bethlehem (Pennsylvania) *Globe*. November 20, 1902.

"Boston University: School of Theology." *Zion's Herald*. June 7, 1893.

Christian Advocate and Journal. June 1957.

Interviews

French, Rebecca. October 22, 1987, Grinnell, Iowa.

Personal and Administrative Correspondence

Boston University Archives. William F. Warren Papers.

Harvard University Archives. Charles W. Eliot Papers.

_____. Harvard Divinity School: Minutes of Faculty Meetings, 1893-1912; 1912-1922.

New York University Archives. MacCracken Administration Papers.

_____. "Proposed Basis or Terms of Voluntary Agreement Between the University of the City of New York and the Union Theological Seminary of the City of New York."

Pacific Palisades, California. Personal Papers of A. Eustace Haydon. In possession of Ethel Haydon.

University of Chicago Archives. Divinity School Correspondence.

_____. Divinity School: Minutes of Faculty Meetings, 1904-1913.

_____. President's Papers: 1889-1925.

_____. William Rainey Harper Papers.

University Publications

Boston University. *Catalogues*. Boston: University Press, 1880-1915.

_____. *Historical Register of Boston University, Fifth Decennial Issue, 1869-1911*. Boston: University Press, 1911.

_____. *Inauguration of Lemuel Herbert Murlin, D.D., L.L.D., as President of Boston University, October 20, 1911*. Boston: University Press, 1911.

_____. *President's Annual Reports*. Boston: University Press, 1880-1915.

Cornell University. *Account of the Proceedings at the Inauguration*. Ithaca: University Press, 1869.

_____. *Annual Reports*. Ithaca: Cornell University Press, 1890-1907.

_____. *Registers*. Ithaca: Cornell University Press, 1890-1907.

Harvard University. *Annual Reports*. Cambridge: University Press, 1867-1933.

_____. *Catalogues*. Cambridge: Harvard University Press, 1867-1935.

_____. *Report of Overseers of Harvard College to Visit the Divinity School*. N.p., 1890-1940.

New York University. *Annual Reports*. New York: University Press, 1885-1930.

_____. *Quadrennial Report of the Chancellor, 1901*. New York: University Press, 1901.

New York University. *University Catalogues*. New York: University Press, 1885-1930.

University of Chicago. *Annual Registers*. Chicago: University Press, 1892-1940.

_____. *Official Publications of the University of Chicago: The Quarterly Calendar*. Chicago: University of Chicago Press, 1894.

_____. *President's Reports*. Chicago: University Press, 1892-1940.

_____. *Register of Doctors of Philosophy, June 1893-April 1936*. Chicago: University of Chicago Press, 1938.

_____. *University of Chicago Official Bulletins, 1891-92*. Chicago: n.p., 1892.

University of Pennsylvania. *Catalogues*. Philadelphia: University Press, 1890-1935.

_____. *Doctors of Philosophy of the Graduate School: 1889-1927*. Philadelphia: University Press, 1890-1935.

_____. *President's Reports*. Philadelphia: University Press, 1890-1935.

Index

163

Chicago Studies in the History of American Religion

Editors

JERALD C. BRAUER & MARTIN E. MARTY

(continued, over)

11. Kountz, Peter. *Thomas Merton as Writer and Monk: A Cultural Study, 1915-1951*

12. Lagerquist, L. DeAne. *In America the Men Milk the Cows: Factors of Gender, Ethnicity, and Religion in the Americanization of Norwegian-American Women*

13. Markwell, Bernard Kent. *The Anglican Left: Radical Social Reformers in the Church of England and the Protestant Episcopal Church, 1846-1954*

14. Morris, William Sparkes. *The Young Jonathan Edwards: A Reconstruction*

15. Pellauer, Mary D. *Toward a Tradition of Feminist Theology: The Religious Social Thought of Elizabeth Cady Stanton, Susan B. Anthony, and Anna Howard Shaw*

16. Potash, P. Jeffrey. *Vermont's Burned-Over District: Patterns of Community Development and Religious Activity, 1761-1850*

17. Queen, Edward L., II. *In the South the Baptists are the Center of Gravity: Southern Baptists and Social Change, 1930-1980*

18. Schmidt, Jean Miller. *Souls or the Social Order: The Two-Party System in American Protestantism*

19. Shaw, Stephen J. *The Catholic Parish as a Way-Station of Ethnicity and Americanization: Chicago's Germans and Italians, 1903-1939*

20. Shepard, Robert S. *God's People in the Ivory Tower: Religion in the Early American University*

21. Snyder, Stephen H. *Lyman Beecher and his Children: The Transformation of a Religious Tradition*